Made To Flourish

Beyond Quick Fixes To A Thriving Organization

Shelley G. Trebesch

16pt

Copyright Page from the Original Book

InterVarsity Press
P.O. Box 1400, Downers Grove, IL 60515-1426
ivpress.com
email@ivpress.com

©2015 by Shelley G. Trebesch

All rights reserved. No part of this book may be reproduced in any form without written permission from InterVarsity Press.

InterVarsity Press® is the book-publishing division of InterVarsity Christian Fellowship/USA®, a movement of students and faculty active on campus at hundreds of universities, colleges and schools of nursing in the United States of America, and a member movement of the International Fellowship of Evangelical Students. For information about local and regional activities, visit intervarsity.org.

Scripture quotations, unless otherwise noted, are from the New Revised Standard Version of the Bible, copyright 1989 by the Division of Christian Education of the National Council of the Churches of Christ in the USA. Used by permission. All rights reserved.

While many stories in this book are true, some names and identifying information may have been changed to protect the privacy of individuals.

Cover design: Cindy Kiple
Interior design: Beth McGill
Images: © AlexRaths/iStockphoto

ISBN 978-0-8308-4440-1 (print)
ISBN 978-0-8308-9895-4 (digital)

Printed in the United States of America ♾

 As a member of the Green Press Initiative, InterVarsity Press is committed to protecting the environment and to the responsible use of natural resources. To learn more, visit greenpressinitiative.org.

Library of Congress Cataloging-in-Publication Data

Trebesch, Shelley G., 1963-
  Made to flourish beyond quick fixes to a thriving organization / Shelley G. Trebesch.
      pages cm
  Includes bibliographical references and index.
  ISBN 978-0-8308-4440-1 (pbk. : alk. paper)
  1. Church management. 2. Organizational effectiveness. I. Title.
  BV652.T687 2015
  254--dc23

2015033681

| P | 23 | 22 | 21 | 20 | 19 | 18 | 17 | 16 | 15 | 14 | 13 | 12 | 11 | 10 | 9 | 8 | 7 | 6 | 5 | 4 | 3 | 2 | 1 |
| Y | 34 | 33 | 32 | 31 | 30 | 29 | 28 | 27 | 26 | 25 | 24 | 23 | 22 | 21 | 20 | 19 | 18 | 17 | 16 | 15 |

TABLE OF CONTENTS

1: A VISION TO FLOURISH	1
2: LANGUISHING OR FLOURISHING?	11
3: THE ECO MODEL AT WORK	28
4: FLOURISHING PEOPLE	36
5: DNA: THE LIFE FORCE OF FLOURISHING ORGANIZATIONS	61
6: PUTTING YOUR DNA TO WORK	82
7: THE DISCIPLINE OF FLOURISHING—ORGANIZATION AND CAPACITY DEVELOPMENT	101
8: MAKING ORGANIZATION DEVELOPMENT WORK FOR YOU	120
9: THE ECOSYSTEM OF FLOURISHING—CULTURE	133
10: MAKING CULTURE WORK FOR YOU	150
11: THE ECOSYSTEM OF FLOURISHING—STRUCTURE	159
12: THE NUTS AND BOLTS OF STRUCTURE	178
13: THE FUTURE OF FLOURISHING—INNOVATION AND ENTREPRENEURS	192
14: FLOURISHING: A DAILY REALITY	213
15: ONE ORGANIZATION'S STORY	231
16: FLOURISHING ORGANIZATIONS	240
ACKNOWLEDGMENTS	253
Appendix 1: TECHNICAL ASPECTS OF FLOURISHING	254
Appendix 2: FLOURISHING DEVELOPMENTAL ASSESSMENT TOOL	259
NOTES	268
Index	287

"*Made to Flourish* provides valuable insights and direction for any organization or church that longs to have a robust, flourishing ministry. Trebesch brings to bear her wealth of experience and research to provide clear, simple concepts for organizational leaders to reflect, evaluate and implement change leading to a flourishing organization. The ecology of organizations model provides a systemic roadmap to develop not just a flourishing organization, but an organization with a life-changing purpose. This book is a must for every organizational leader!"

Geri Rodman, president, Inter-Varsity Christian Fellowship of Canada

"Shelley Trebesch has a rare gift—she is able to combine her understanding of the technical, academic grasp of this great subject with the practical application she has shared with companies small and large. She empowers readers to be in the right conversations, asking the right questions in order the find the right solutions for their journeys. This is most helpful when theories swirl around without being anchored in the daily trenches of leadership."

Chris Wienand, copastor, Mercy Town Church, president, Genesis Collective, catalyst, The Global Project

"*Made to Flourish* is a powerful handbook for thoughtful organizational leaders who care about results *and* building environments where people thrive. Trebesch does a masterful job presenting solutions for leaders to lead people well through any change or organization development initiative."

Santiago "Jimmy" Mellado, president and CEO, Compassion International

"Made to Flourish brings clarity and understanding to the mysteries and complexity of organizational leadership. It is written with simplicity and a fine combination of leadership and organizational theory, blended with rich case studies in the contemporary context to illustrate how flourishing organizations can be developed. A thought-provoking book that will encourage leaders to transform organizations beyond the quick fixes."

Patrick Fung, general director, OMF International

"Organizations are made to flourish, yet too many languish due to a lack of understanding. Shelley Trebesch gives us of years of wisdom by introducing us to a dynamic, holistic, practical and time-tested tool that she calls the ECO model. She makes the complex comprehensible. I'll be using this tool in my work with church planters."

JR Woodward, author of *Creating a Missional Culture*

To Mom and Dad,

who help me pursue flourishing.

A VISION TO FLOURISH

Focus on Unreached Peoples (FUP) began when eight university graduates sensed God's call to pray for, research and plant churches among unreached peoples. The organization grew steadily, eventually numbering four hundred people (along with support staff) serving in fifteen creative-access nations.

Thirty years into the work, FUP experienced a 25 percent decrease in all areas of the organization (personnel, finances, new frontiers, etc.). The decline began when forty missionaries living in two neighboring African countries were forced to evacuate due to civil war. Two missionaries were killed in the conflict before they were able to leave the country.

The thirty-eight missionaries were immediately redeployed, although some chose to leave the mission due to the trauma. Other missionaries were given assignments within the organization—mostly in leadership and administration—and some were reassigned to safer countries with strong Christian presences (mostly to offer support to already-existing churches). The civil war was rarely spoken of again; everyone seemed to forget and move on. As the personnel and resources in the organization continued to decline, the leadership made decisions to consolidate and assigned the few new workers to contexts where there were already personnel. They didn't start work in any new countries.

Contributions continued to decrease along with the operating budget. Support staff were laid off. Missionary budgets had not been increased for ten years. The atmosphere in the organization was tense. Most sensed and promoted attitudes of scarcity, comparison and begrudged sharing, noticing "who got what." Of course, everyone felt they did not have enough—and they probably didn't.

New initiatives focused on fundraising and training staff for effective support development. Five years into the decline, the board hired a new CEO who had a track record for generating income. He did, but by this point morale was so low, money could not resolve the situation.

Here was a classic leadership challenge: the law of unintended, unexpected consequences. Obviously the well-intentioned organizational leaders of FUP needed to act quickly for the safety of the missionaries caught in the midst of civil war. Did they realize, however, that they were employing a quick fix? That their redeployment interventions would have the overall, long-term impact of a 25 percent decrease in all areas of mission and potentially jeopardize the vision for which FUP exists? That the impact of the redeployment of the trusted partners of the African nationals would be betrayal and distrust? That their financial partners would become skeptical and invest elsewhere?

> **Stop and Think**
> Consider your organization or team. Try to identify some "quick fixes" and notice their repercussions, their ripple effects.

Often, leaders initiate change in their organizations or teams as a reaction to an event, a response to crisis. New policies are written or new structures implemented with minimal projection toward consequences or future outcomes. Another common approach is for leaders to search for breakthroughs and pursue the latest fads, the strategies that seem to work in the "church down the street." Many organizational changes happen in response to the symptoms of events—what is easily observable or seen. As previously stated, these are quick fixes. If an organization is to flourish, it has to go beyond quick fixes. It has to see more deeply and listen more intently.

MADE TO FLOURISH

What does it mean to flourish?[1] One definition is "to live within an optimal range of human functioning, one that connotes goodness, generativity, growth, and resilience."[2] Not surprisingly, the opening chapters of Genesis also offer a sense of what flourishing means.

> Then God said, "Let the earth put forth vegetation: plants yielding seed, and fruit trees of every kind on earth that bear fruit with the seed in it." And it was so.... And God said, "Let the waters bring forth swarms of living creatures, and let birds fly above the earth across the dome of the sky." ... Then God said, "Let us make humankind in our image, according to our likeness; and let them have dominion over the fish of the sea, and over the birds of the air, and over the cattle, and over all the wild animals of the earth, and over every creeping thing that creeps upon the earth." ... God blessed them, and God said to them, "Be fruitful and multiply, and fill the earth and subdue it; and have dominion over the fish of the sea and over the birds of the air and over every living thing that moves upon the earth." (Gen 1:11, 20, 26, 28)

Jesus also envisions flourishing in Luke's Gospel when he references Isaiah 61:1-2.

> The Spirit of the Lord is upon me,
> because he has anointed me
> to bring good news to the poor.
> He has sent me to proclaim release to the captives
> and recovery of sight to the blind,

> to let the oppressed go free,
> to proclaim the year of the Lord's favor.
> (Lk 4:18-19)

Flourishing is also our ultimate hope as pictured in the book of Revelation.

> Then I saw a new heaven and a new earth; for the first heaven and the first earth had passed away, and the sea was no more....
> "See, the home of God is among mortals.
> He will dwell with them;
> they will be his peoples,
> and God himself will be with them;
> he will wipe every tear from their eyes.
> Death will be no more;
> mourning and crying and pain will be no more,
> for the first things have passed away." (Rev 21:1, 3-4)

God created the world and all of us in it to flourish. Jesus came to restore flourishing to a broken world and to point us in that direction before God finally rights all wrongs and accomplishes fully what he initially set out to do at creation.

When we flourish, we experience emotional, psychological and social well-being. We are full of life—peaceful, cheerful, satisfied and productive.[3] We accept ourselves as we are, knowing our strengths and weaknesses. We engage challenges, enjoy learning and embrace an overall sense of purpose. We expect our days to be useful and hopeful. Flourishing people have strong relationships and connectedness to community, contributing as well as receiving. They are curious about differences and suspend judgment for optimized learning. Sound appealing? Sound like what God might intend life to be?

Humans—created in God's image—are meant to flourish, and in that flourishing, they learn and become cocreators with God.[4] In flourishing environments, we pursue meaning and purpose. We innovate and adapt to adjust in new situations or when faced with challenges. Organizations oriented toward the kingdom of God, whether churches, NGOs, mission agencies, other nonprofits or businesses, ultimately should flourish. In other words, in a flourishing organization or team, everything and everyone is thriving.[5]

What does that look like? Organizations are communities of people called together for a purpose. Christian organizations—churches and companies—exist for the greater purposes of God's kingdom. They live and work in God's freedom-producing, life-giving, holistic reign, experiencing the wildness, adventure, fruitfulness and abundant life of God's kingdom while inviting others to do so as well.

Flourishing organizations are thrilling in that they pursue meaningful, kingdom-of-God-oriented purposes. They make a difference in society and individual lives. A called community that participates in God's mission is unique. The way it participates in the kingdom and partners with God for kingdom purposes is as individual as human beings themselves, and it must live this uniqueness to demonstrate the full breadth of God's image. Ultimately, Christian organizations should be flourishing and thriving because that reflects their Creator's image.

Flourishing organizations are
- vibrant, reproducing, kingdom-of-God communities
- called together to live in God's reign and join God's mission to proclaim and live in his kingdom and to, by God's enabling grace,
- pursue their unique, God-given purpose and
- produce God's vision of the future
- while creating an environment where individuals thrive.

Flourishing organizations are fun, satisfying, safe environments in which individuals are restored and embrace transformation into the image of Christ. They live the authentic Jesus life—attractive, joyful, contagious.

QUICK FIXES

All too often, however, that's not how leaders think about organizations, especially when problems or crises arise. That's what happened to the leaders of FUP. Their approach of using quick fixes is all too common. They rapidly employed reactionary solutions to correct a situation. Quick fixes by definition lack research and analysis and therefore a deep awareness of the complexity inherent in every organization, department or team. Ronald Heifitz and Marty Linsky call these technical changes or solutions because they are based on know-how that already exists.[6] Quick fixes may give the initial appearance of relieving the problem in the context of crisis, but in a matter of time the same (or new) problems surface again.

Quick fixes are often faddish. We see a strategy working in another organization, so we are tempted to try it out in our own context—even though our situation may be very different. As a result, the outcome is often disappointing. Researchers working with Jim Collins found that "no single defining action, no grand program, no one killer innovation, no solitary lucky break, no miracle moment" would lead an organization to greatness.[7] Therefore, the hard work of comprehensive research and discernment is necessary before leaders intervene with organizational change.

Another issue can make it difficult for organizations to flourish. After over twenty-five years of starting, leading, growing and consulting in numerous organizations, often internationally, I continually see leaders with little, if any, leadership training. Rather, they are called to captain their organizations or teams because of their character and frontline experience in other contexts. Full of good intentions and a lot of energy, such leaders still find their troubles outweighing their successes. The complexities of the venture can be overwhelming.

Made to Flourish brings to light the mysteries and complexities of organizational leadership and offers overall perspective for those who lead organizations who want to accomplish kingdom-of-God purposes. *Made to Flourish* encourages "adaptive leadership, ... the practice of mobilizing people to tackle tough challenges and thrive."[8]

The structure of *Made to Flourish* is straightforward and can be read as a whole or in parts based on the challenges you face. Chapter two introduces a model (the Ecology of Organizations, ECO) for flourishing organizations, while subsequent chapters explore the components of this model in-depth. Beyond chapter two, each chapter includes three elements: (1) live case studies that illustrate common quick fixes, (2) presentations of an aspect of organizational dynamics that promotes flourishing, and (3) effective best practices and exercises related to the dynamic being explored.

It is my prayer that *Made to Flourish* will help you and your teams listen and think deeply about your organization, beyond the quick fixes, and thus call forth life. It is my hope that as a result your organization will flourish.

2

LANGUISHING OR FLOURISHING?

Predicting the Ripple Effects of Change

Campus by the Sea, a camping facility run by InterVarsity Christian Fellowship on Catalina Island off the coast of Southern California, had a problem.[1] Rattlesnakes had been on the island for time out of mind. In the mid-1930s, some enterprising folk brought in wild pigs to keep the snake population under control. The plan worked great. Fewer snakes.

But then the wild pigs started to roam all over, invading campgrounds and other areas. So some enterprising folk used a dog, Cinder, to keep the pigs at bay. The plan worked great. Fewer pigs.

But Cinder left lots of little presents lying around, making things very unpleasant for guests at the campground. So some workers were given the task of cleaning up after the dog. The plan worked great. Fewer little presents from Cinder for people to step in.

But then the pigs got the better of Cinder. Within weeks of Cinder's retirement, the pigs were back.

All of this took place over the course of decades, with each group of leaders not fully aware of what previous groups had done before to solve the problems. Many lessons could be learned from this tale, I'm sure, not the least of which is that a judicious knowledge of the history of your enterprise can come in handy. It also illustrates the law of unintended consequences. We fail to foresee what might result from certain decisions we make.

Figure 2.1. Direct cause and effect

Organizational leaders, especially from the West, tend to view events as linear cause and effect (see figure 2.1).[2] Educational systems have taught them that a cause produces an effect. In reality, however, the effect becomes another cause, which produces another effect. This produces another cause, which produces another effect and so on. Like the problem at Campus by the Sea with the snakes that produced a problem with pigs that produced a problem with a dog, events are never purely linear—an effect becomes a cause and then an effect, in more of a circular fashion. In systems thinking, this is called a cause-effect loop (see figure 2.2).

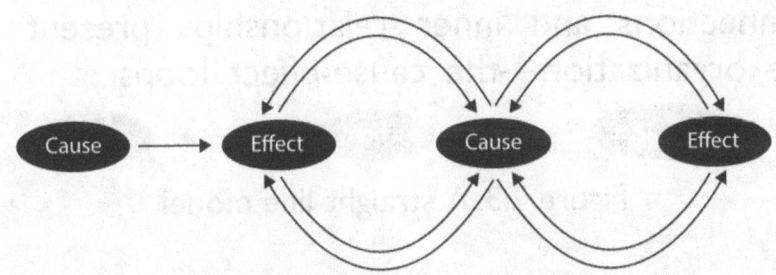

Figure 2.2. A cause-effect loop

When we receive information about an experience that indicates a need for change, we take actions, which produce particular results. But reality is not linear as figure 2.3 portrays. New information based on the results leads to actions, which lead to further results. It's more like a circle than a straight line, more like a never-ending spiral. More like figure 2.4. When we analyze in a systems mindset, reality encompasses the past, present and future.

As we know, only 10 percent of an iceberg is above water; 90 percent is below. Likewise, when we analyze an event, we must discern the unseen interrelationships and connections, keeping in mind the past and present, and projecting toward the future. To move beyond quick fixes toward flourishing (that is, effective growth, change and development), organizational leaders must seek to reveal and understand the 90 percent of the organization that is below the surface, beyond the obvious events. To prevent quick fixes, they must understand the inner connections and inner relationships present in the organization—the cause-effect loops.

Figure 2.3. A straight-line model

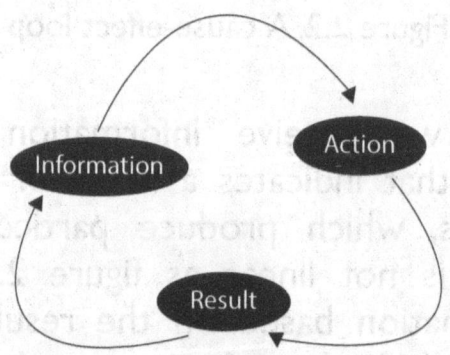

Figure 2.4. A circular model

The model I present in this book for understanding these loops and the 90 percent below the surface is called the Ecology of Organizations (ECO). It shows inner relationships and connectedness so that leaders can trace influence and predict repercussions. That's how we move away from quick fixes. I use the word *ecology* to convey that the cause-effect nature of organizations is, by definition, *organic* and not mechanical. Organizations are not machines. You don't pull a lever at one end and get a gizmo at the other. Organizations are active, dynamic *organisms* that need nurture and care, that are affected by both their DNA and by their environment. Organizations entail many complex, interactive processes that are often not easily quantifiable.

Yet even in growing and changing organisms like plants and animals, there are repeated cycles of growth, producing fruit and dormancy—or of birth, growth and death. Likewise, following the connections in cause-effect loops is a process we can repeat, enabling us to observe, interpret and intervene, which is the essential process of adaptive leadership.[3]

Regarding FUP (Focus on Unreached Peoples) that we met in chapter one, for example, what impact did the change in organizational structure (redeployment) have on its vision and mission? Did the structural change promote or hinder the vision? Did the change align with FUP's values? How did the change in policy (redeployment to safer countries) affect the morale or experience of members in the organization? Or of the Africans who remained in their home countries during the turmoil? Did it enable them to flourish and participate meaningfully in the mission? As a good garden needs the right balance of ingredients (water, soil, sunlight, fertilizer, weed control and more), so a flourishing organization requires the right balance of ingredients, each of which is a cause-effect loop of constant movement and feedback.

VISION AND MISSION

In the rest of this chapter I will build the ECO model piece by piece until we have the whole. We will then look at each of the pieces in more detail in subsequent chapters.

Let's start then with the first piece, the vision and mission loop (figure 2.5). This lies in the center, at the heart of the organization. Mission and vision impact everything that happens in the organization. At the same time, what happens in the organization also impacts the mission and vision. It is not just one way. For example, structural changes without reference to the mission and vision of an organization may impact them negatively and over time cause the mission and/or vision to drift. The organization may not accomplish the outcomes for which it exists. In chapter five I will say much more about vision and mission, helping distinguish these two terms that are sometimes equated with one another. But I don't want to slow us down with that at the moment. Let's move on to the next piece of the ECO model.

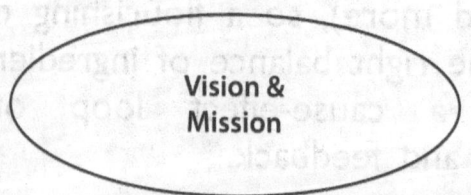

Figure 2.5. The vision and mission loop

INTERNAL PARADIGMS

The next cause-effect loop consists of faith assumptions and values, what I call the internal paradigms loop because it represents controlling mindsets that inevitably influence decision making and actions (see figure 2.6). These are the unseen (internal) factors that influence external actions. Faith assumptions are biblical and theological truths that provide foundation for the organization and influence organizational decision making and actions. Examples might include the following:

- God transforms lives.
- Individuals contribute to the whole by using their gifts.
- All people/nations must have the opportunity to hear the gospel.

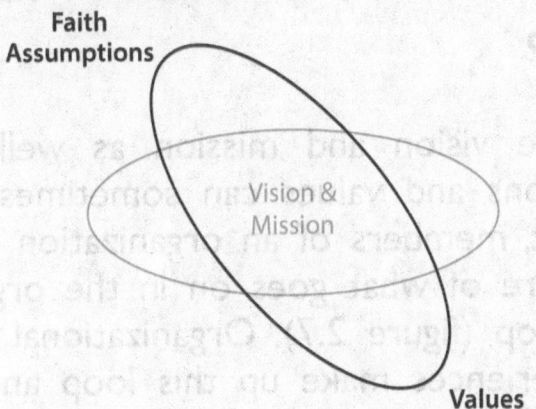

Figure 2.6. The internal paradigms loop

Values are standards or principles that cause us to make decisions or act the way we do. They describe what matters most: the kind of people we are, the type of work we do and how we behave as we do the work. They determine our behavior—and, as we'll see in the coming sections, our behaviors influence our values.

In terms of the movement in the cause-effect loop, faith assumptions tend to create, produce, strengthen and influence values. Likewise, values have similar effects on faith assumptions. This sometimes hidden cause-effect loop affects people, for example, more visibly through policies and procedures. Chapter five will discuss in more detail how this loop interacts with the vision and mission loop.

THE ORGANIZATION ACTION LOOP

While vision and mission as well as faith assumptions and values can sometimes be hard to detect, members of an organization are often very aware of what goes on in the organization action loop (figure 2.7). Organizational dynamics and experiences make up this loop and include policies, procedures, governance, structure and the like. These enable an organization to function efficiently and accomplish its purpose. Policies and procedures might include the following:

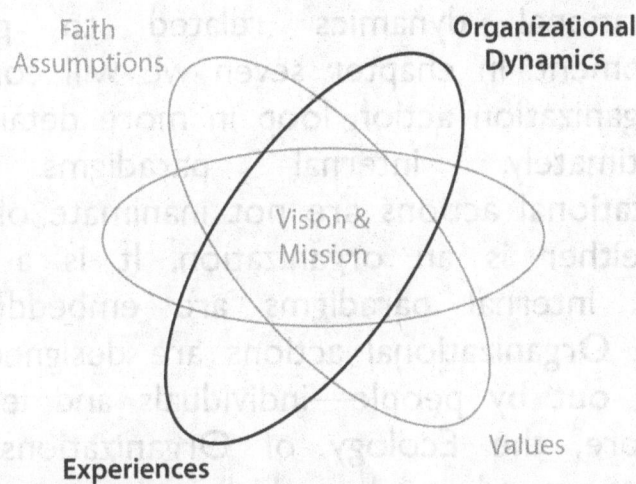

Figure 2.7. The organization action loop

- Assessments—evaluation, feedback and plans for development regarding people's work
- Human resources policies
- Budget and planning processes
- Delivery of ministry or services

These dynamics then influence the other part of the loop: the experiences of people. These are the events and practices that influence and shape people within organizations. For example, suppose an organization has an effective overall development and training process that includes thorough orientation, initial training that equips members to do the mission and accomplish the vision, yearly developmental reviews and planning, and ongoing training that further develops and refines members in their selected career paths. Presumably then, members experience growth and development, which further strengthens the organizational dynamics related to people development. In chapter seven we will consider the organization action loop in more detail.

Ultimately, internal paradigms and organizational actions are not inanimate objects, and neither is an organization. It is a living system. Internal paradigms are embedded in people. Organizational actions are designed and carried out by people—individuals and leaders. Therefore, the Ecology of Organizations fully connects around people—which is the cause-effect loop highlighted next.

THE PEOPLE LOOP

We began by saying that vision and mission are at the center of the organization. In purposeful, flourishing organizations, leaders and individuals connect with and live the vision and mission (see figure 2.8). Vision and mission are not just nice statements printed on posters. They are the reasons for which God called the organization into existence. Therefore, vision and mission should be innate aspects of every member of an organization. However, consider the cause-effect aspect of the loop. If leaders and individuals do not live the vision and mission, if they do not replicate the vision and mission in new generations, over time the vision and mission will change and so will, inevitably, the organization. This "drift" may propel the organization into a state where it exists for itself but not its God-given purpose.

Figure 2.8. The people loop

J. Robert "Bobby" Clinton defines leadership as "a dynamic process in which a man or woman with God-given capacity influences a specific group of God's people toward His purposes for the group."[4] Leaders are influenced by the organization's vision, mission, faith assumptions and values. As a result they create experiences and organizational dynamics. These in turn influence individuals and strengthen or establish faith assumptions, values, vision and mission. Leaders are key in organizations since their actions (flowing from faith assumptions and values) create organizational culture, structures, procedures, policies and so forth. They are often the initiators of experiences that cause individuals in the organization to grow and develop.

Individuals have an effect on the loop too. In healthy organizations, change is initiated by the grassroots as well as by the leaders. When people are influenced by the organization's vision, mission, faith assumptions and values, they then create organizational dynamics and experiences that influence leaders. That in turn strengthens or establishes their vision, mission, values and faith assumptions. The cause-effect loop flows in both directions, and individuals and leaders both influence the whole organization.

Often those in difficult situations who are not in leadership feel powerless to affect their situation or bring change to the whole. However, in a living organism, every part influences the whole. As Paul said in 1 Corinthians 12,

> The body does not consist of one member but of many. If the foot would say, "Because I am not a hand, I do not belong to the body," that would not make it any less a part of the body. And if the ear would say, "Because I am not an eye, I do not belong to the body," that would not make it any less a part of the body. If the whole body were an eye, where would the hearing be? If the whole body were hearing, where would the sense of smell be? But as it is, God arranged the members in the body, each one of them, as he chose. If all were a single member, where would the body be? As it is, there are many members, yet one body. The eye cannot say to the

hand, "I have no need of you," nor again the head to the feet, "I have no need of you." On the contrary, the members of the body that seem to be weaker are indispensable, and those members of the body that we think less honorable we clothe with greater honor, and our less respectable members are treated with greater respect; whereas our more respectable members do not need this. But God has so arranged the body, giving the greater honor to the inferior member, that there may be no dissension within the body, but the members may have the same care for one another. If one member suffers, all suffer together with it; if one member is honored, all rejoice together with it. (1 Cor 12:14-26)

The ECO model (figure 2.9) reveals connections and demonstrates that even a small change or life-producing action infuses the whole organization—even when people feel they have no power or cannot readily observe their influence.

Figure 2.9. The Ecology of Organizations (ECO) model

CONTEXT

Admittedly, introducing the ECO model in a book has two-dimensional limitations. But imagine the picture as three-dimensional, interlocking, interinfluencing loops, much like a gyroscope. All the loops connect to and influence the whole. What happens in one loop impacts all the loops, the whole, like a child's hanging mobile. This "whole" represents an organization—with its people (leaders and individuals), mission, vision, faith assumptions, values, organizational dynamics (structure, policies and procedures) and the rest.

Of course the organization exists in a context; therefore, not only do the parts (the inner cause-effect loops) influence the whole, the context influences the organization and the organization influences the context (yes, another cause-effect loop!). Influences, of course, can either be positive, negative or neutral. Economic downturns, natural disasters and government regulations, all beyond an organization's control, nonetheless impact the organization and require the organization's response. As we saw in chapter one, a civil war in two neighboring African countries dramatically influenced FUP. Figure 2.10 shows the ECO model in its environment.

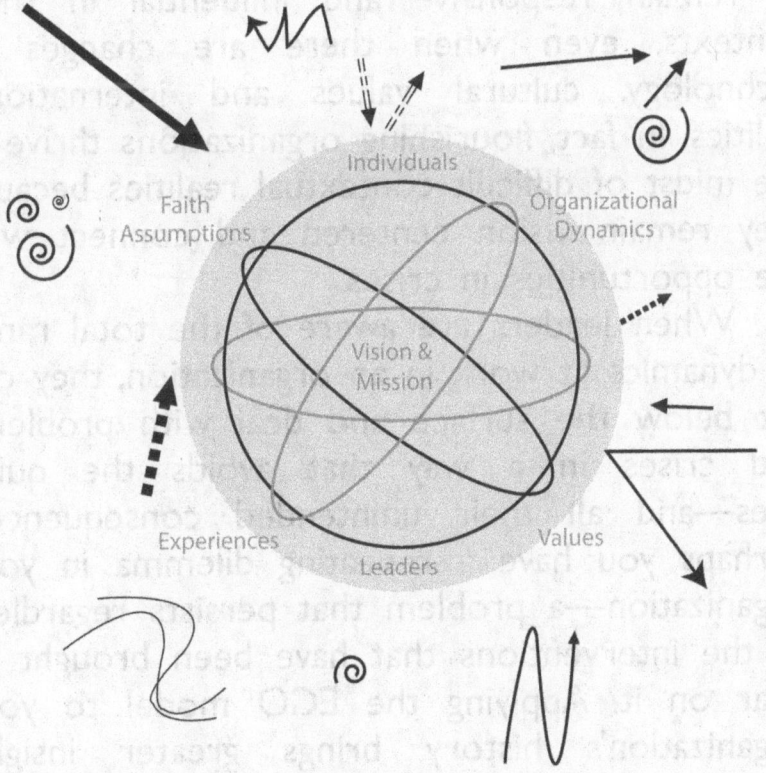

Figure 2.10. The influence of environment on an organization

That organizations exist in a particular context is a given, a fact. The level of connection between the environment and the organization, however, depends on the organization and particularly on its DNA (mission, vision, faith assumptions and values—to be addressed in chapter five) and therefore, practices. Growing, reproducing—that is, flourishing—organizations deeply connect with their contexts so as to bear witness to the kingdom of God in a way that matters. They flex, innovate and adapt in order to remain responsive and influential in their contexts, even when there are changes in technology, cultural values and international politics. In fact, flourishing organizations thrive in the midst of difficult contextual realities because they remain vision centered and connect with the opportunities in crises.

When leaders are aware of the total range of dynamics at work in an organization, they can get below the surface and deal with problems and crises in a way that avoids the quick fixes—and all their unintended consequences. Perhaps you have a repeating dilemma in your organization—a problem that persists regardless of the interventions that have been brought to bear on it. Applying the ECO model to your organization's history brings greater insight, allowing you to understand the inner dynamics, which may suggest more fruitful interventions.

Stop and Think

Take a minute to note down problems in your organization that persist regardless of applied interventions. Regarding the problem, which cause-effect loop seems to be most in play? Notice this loop's connectedness to the other loops in the ECO model. How are they affected?

This chapter has had a lot to absorb in a short span, but I wanted to give an overview of where we were going before we looked in depth at each of the parts. Before we do that, however, let's take a look at how the ECO model applies in the case study we've been considering—Focus on Unreached Peoples. That's what's ahead in the next chapter.

3
THE ECO MODEL AT WORK

Because the civil war made for an unsafe situation, the leaders of Focus on Unreached Peoples (FUP), which we were introduced to in chapter one, redeployed workers in safer countries with strong Christian presences. When revenue fell, they then consolidated personnel and ceased opening up work in new countries. Hoping to reverse the decline in personnel and funding, eventually staff received more training for support development.

All of these changes were quick fixes that didn't look into deeper issues. More than that, going back to figure 2.10, we can see that all the changes the leaders made were also part of the organizational dynamics and experiences cause-effect loop. They made structural and training changes, none of which were effective in stopping the decline.

The board made one more intervention, however. It hired a new CEO, part of the people cause-effect loop. It seems, however, that this intervention likely would not help the organization get back on track because of the reasons for which the CEO was hired—to generate income, not to address the vision, mission, faith assumptions and values. We don't know whether the new CEO had the organization's DNA; it may have even been difficult to know what the DNA was at this point in its crisis-clouded history. Inherently he did, however, have his own faith assumptions and values, which would have had an overall effect on FUP.

What would have happened if organizational leaders had used the ECO model or paused to analyze the ripple effects of their decision making on the whole organization and its future?

Let's begin by analyzing the first intervention, the redeployment of missionaries in safer, already Christianized countries. This became something of a long-term strategy. The leadership didn't consider how this change in structure and strategy might affect other cause-effect loops. They failed to ask what impact the decision would have on the mission "to pray for, research and plant churches among unreached peoples." Nor did they consider what the decision revealed about the organization's faith assumptions and values. Had those assumptions and values changed in a way that led to the redeployment decision? Did the organizational leaders anticipate the ripple effects (cause-effect loops) their decisions would have on various contexts, such as the locals in the two African nations they had worked in as well as the prayer and financial partners connected to the forty missionaries?

When the first intervention brought less-than-satisfying results, other interventions were made in organizational dynamics and finally in the people loop by hiring a new CEO. All interventions addressed surface issues, the events easily observable and easily changed. Yet the deeper issues of mission and vision—for what and for whom did FUP exist?—and faith assumptions and values remained unexamined in the crisis and in the years to come.

While the FUP case study is fictional, it demonstrates all-too-common propensities in organizations. First, FUP did not replicate its DNA, by which I mean the combination of faith assumptions and values along with vision and mission (something we'll look at in more detail in chapter five). God calls organizations and communities into existence for a purpose. This purpose must be fulfilled. This story must be told. The mission, vision, faith assumptions and values must be passed on to new generations. If that DNA is lost, the organization ceases to flourish.

Second, not surprisingly, the superficial or reactive decisions—the quick fixes—just didn't work. Insightful and effective interventions require analysis and study of the repercussions of decisions. We must understand the effects in every aspect of the organization and project these effects toward the future. The purpose of this book is to unpack the ECO model, because I have seen how helpful it can be in facilitating this process.

ANTICIPATING CHANGE

While many changes in the organizational context are straightforward and make use of well-known solutions, other changes require deeper research, collaboration and experiments in order to address adaptive challenges.[1] The ECO model helps us understand inner dynamics so we can apply adaptive solutions—changes that can affect the whole organization in fundamental, positive ways.

Practically speaking, many factors may indicate a need for organizational change; for example, the need to respond to opportunities related to the vision, implementing new strategies that can enable the mission to be achieved, or the presence of cumbersome procedures that block efficient and effective pursuit of the vision.

Acme Christian University began eighty years ago as a mission school focused on sending people overseas to plant churches and establish hospitals.[2] That bent toward activism has continued to be part of the fabric of the institution even as it has grown into a full-fledged university. Teachers and staff have been attracted to the university because its mission and ethos are active and productive. Everyone works long hours, accomplishes a lot and is energized by the camaraderie of the work. But now the HR department has reported to the administration that in the last four years there has been a marked increase in attrition.

What should the administration do? A quick fix would be to increase efforts in recruitment that may help fill the empty slots in the short term. They could add a "Careers at Acme Christian University" page to their website or start an internship program for graduates or liaise with mission agencies to connect with missionaries returning from the field. But the ECO model shows other cause-effect loops may need to be addressed.

First, attrition happens in the cause-effect loop related to organizational dynamics and experiences. So the administration could ask, What are employees experiencing that causes them to leave? How, if at all, are these experiences connected to organizational dynamics such as structure or training or supervision (all of which are connected to the leaders/individuals cause-effect loop as well)?

They should then go deeper and connect these experiences to the university's faith assumptions and values. Do the espoused values of the university match the actual policies and practices of the leadership? Do some people just find it too difficult at some point to live up to these values? Or is it that the actual values don't match the espoused values in some ways? Regarding faith assumptions, how do the long hours and activism connect with their theology?

Is there a sense that employees must work harder and longer in order to be "good" Christians?

What did the administration of Acme actually do? They conducted third-party exit interviews and focus groups of employees to see what further could be uncovered. When they focused on the internal paradigms cause-effect loop, they discovered works-oriented faith assumptions underneath. People felt valued in the organization by what they accomplished or how busy their schedule was. In fact, the "hero" stories of the organization usually related to busyness—working through weekends or thirteen-hour days, never taking a vacation or sick day. The interviews also revealed feelings of being judged. Those who had left felt they just weren't strong enough or that they lacked the faith needed to be a productive member of the staff.

Inadvertently, Acme had slowly changed from a culture of joyful activity animated by the Spirit to one of busyness driven by guilt. The values they espoused no longer matched their actual values. Sheer industriousness had gradually ceased to be enough to inspire and motivate people. Teachers and staff at Acme were not valued and developed as bearers of God's image, and eventually they became worn out or burned out and left the organization.

Rather than solely changing the cause-effect loop related to organizational dynamics and experiences (e.g., increased recruitment), Acme decided that faith assumptions and values needed to be evaluated and reworked first. This would in turn lead to changes in organizational dynamics and experiences.

The university began to revise its previously restrictive sabbatical policy. Until this point, sabbaticals had only been granted for field experience, contributing to a church-planting team or visiting hospitals. Now employees could take sabbaticals for their own developmental goals and even refreshment. Having discovered that the staff had not been regularly taking their full vacation allotment each year, they trained supervisors to make sure employees knew the university wanted them to get the rest and refreshment they needed. The administration ensured that the supervisors took their vacations to model this new approach.

In addition, employees were told to take off one day a week with full pay during the summer months, which tended to be less demanding. Acme also began increasing opportunities for training and development. They sought to create new career paths to engage employees over the long haul. The various interventions had the overall effect of shifting the faith assumptions and values of Acme toward more sustainable and healthy lifestyles. And they paid off. Five years later, HR reported a decrease in attrition.

Often our interventions in organizations address symptoms or superficial issues, but in the end they do not stick, because we have not seen the deeper connections and inner-relationships, and therefore, we do not understand real, transformative change. Here is a process for seeing the 90 percent below the surface. That's the ECO model at work.

4
FLOURISHING PEOPLE

Africa Future, a community development organization working in ten African countries, advertised for a new chief financial officer. When discussing the position, job description and potential candidates with the search committee, the founder lamented,

We cannot trust Africans with money. Last year one of the African managers "borrowed" organizational money for a family member in the hospital. The year before, another manager falsified receipts and stole money. Therefore, we instituted strict policies regarding how managers handle petty cash and expense reimbursement. That solved some of our missing cash issues, but then earlier this year, we found another manager receiving kickbacks from several vendors, so we created more rules. Yet the policies do not prevent infractions. These people just cannot be in charge of money, and we need someone from the outside to exercise more stringent control over our finances.[1]

Based on the founder's wishes, the search committee began looking for a non-African, someone from either Europe or North America.

We may be shocked at the evident racism of the Africa Future founder, but further analysis may reveal other important factors regarding his faith assumptions about human beings and organizations. Here are a few to consider. First, in the founder's mind, some cultures are more trustworthy than others—perhaps because of their wealth, education, the societies from which they originate (i.e., "corrupt" vs. "not corrupt") or just due to the founder's own ethnocentrism. Second, he is apparently working on the assumption that workers must be controlled with strict regulations and policies. Otherwise, when given the opportunity, they will take advantage of the organization. Third, the founder sees rules and regulations, rather than environments of transformation and processes for equipping, as the means to ensure control of behavior in organizations.

Here's a situation from another organization. Adam and his team were having lunch with Max, the company CEO, and the senior leadership team.[2] The previous week Max had interrupted the work of Adam's team on a new line of furniture. Max gathered the team and asked for innovative ideas for how their work environment and operations could improve. At the time, the team was so surprised to see the CEO on the factory floor, they could not offer any new ideas. They mostly expressed gratitude to Max and the other leaders for creating a company that welcomed their contributions and enabled them to share in the profits each year. They knew that their work was significant.

The team talked after Max left, however, and realized that if they restructured the production line, it would enable more collaborative work and thus further increase quality, which was already the industry standard. They also sensed that their results would increase if the designers and engineers were more a part of the collaboration. They scheduled a meeting with Max and the senior leaders to discuss restructuring the factory layout so that the designers' and engineers' offices would be on the factory floor together.

As Adam's team proposed the new layout at the lunch with Max, the energy in the room was palpable. One idea sparked another and then built on another, until all the leaders and team members arrived at solutions that really could change the way they worked and release more creativity. Knowing that the team and leaders were only a small part of the company, however, Max decided to have them present their collaborative ideas to the other teams and collect more data before the redesign took place.

What were the faith assumptions, the theological underpinnings, in this situation? What did the leaders believe about human beings and their participation in organizations? In my interviews with Max De Pree, he stated that at Herman Miller they view each person as someone who contributes to the mission and success of the company and as someone who wants to grow. Each person, because we are all made in the image of God, offers creativity and knowledge for how things can be better. That is why the company has a policy of profit sharing from which every person in the company benefits.

The different assumptions at Africa Future and Herman Miller radically affected how and if people flourished and whether each organization fulfilled its mission. If leaders assume they need to control and design a machine-like organization (like the founder of Africa Future), those in the organization will feel like "cogs"—lifeless and replaceable parts—and therefore lack a sense of real purpose and contribution. On the other hand, people in life-oriented organizations—flourishing organizations—know they contribute to the overall mission and that their work makes a difference. At the same time they experience their own growth and transformation into the image of Christ.

LANGUISHING OR FLOURISHING PEOPLE?

People—individuals and leaders—shaped by faith assumptions and values, pursue the organization's vision and carry out the mission (see figure 4.1). In doing so, they create organizational dynamics, which as a result shape the experiences people have in an organization.

I suspect that most of us have not thought a lot about our theology of organizations—much less put it in writing. We naturally operate in our churches, NGOs and agencies based on what we have experienced in the past, without realizing the connection between our theology and what we do. In this chapter we'll look at a robust theology of the Trinity and of humans as God's image bearers. This offers foundational assumptions that make flourishing organizations possible. The point I'll be driving home along the way is this: Ultimately, flourishing people produce flourishing organizations.

Figure 4.1. The people loop

I quoted from Genesis 1 earlier. It is so foundational that it's worth repeating here:

> Then God said, "Let us make humankind in our image, according to our likeness; and let them have dominion over

the fish of the sea, and over the birds of the air, and over the cattle, and over all the wild animals of the earth, and over every creeping thing that creeps upon the earth."
So God created humankind in his image, in the image of God he created them; male and female he created them.

God blessed them, and God said to them, "Be fruitful and multiply, and fill the earth and subdue it; and have dominion over the fish of the sea and over the birds of the air and over every living thing that moves upon the earth." (Gen 1:26-28)

Flourishing is the designed essence of all living beings. Human beings are created in God's image to be fruitful and multiply. They represent "the cosmos's Creator" and participate as regents of creation, that is, God-appointed leaders and stewards of creation.[3] In effect, we are co-creators, not of the physical universe, of course, but creators nonetheless as we imaginatively develop new ideas and ways of stewarding so that all living beings flourish. God creates us to be agents of flourishing and therefore to shape environments and organizations for the purpose of flourishing.

Stop and Think

> Take a minute to write down your thoughts to these questions:
> - How would you describe your theology of organizations?
> - What is your view of human beings?
> - When you think of people working in your organization, what comes to mind?
> - What is your theology of humans?

As a sermon I heard referencing Genesis 3 put it, "the enemy tries to shrink our vision and focuses us on one tree; one tree when all of creation needs care and when we are meant to be fruitful and multiply."[4] The enemy tries to stunt us through bondage and death, whether in prejudice, suspicion, broken relationships or misuse of creation. And unfortunately, many times our leadership and organizational contexts provide the chains of confinement.

GOD'S IMAGE: UNITY AND CONNECTEDNESS

The ECO model is not just a nice way of thinking about organizations. Connectedness is how humans are created in God's image. It is the actual way we exist in the world. Beyond being co-creators and regents of creation, being created in God's image implies connectedness. God's essence exists in the unity and love of three persons: Father, Son and Spirit. "Relational personhood, which characterizes the inner life of the Father, Son, and Holy Spirit, is fundamental to human personhood as well. Because we're made in the image of the triune God."[5] The very essence of being human is personal (offering and receiving each person's individuality) and relational. "To be a person is to be made in the image of God: that is the heart of the matter. If God is a communion of persons inseparably related, then ... it is in our relatedness to others that our being human consists."[6] It follows then that flourishing organizations foster connection and unity.[7]

Augustine's premise was that God is love and God is Trinity—three persons in perfect unity—"he that loves, and that which is loved, and love."[8] Martin Buber, an early twentieth-century theologian who directed conversations back to the Trinity, took Augustine's ideas and reaffirmed the personalness and relationality of God. Humans and God function in an "I-Thou" relationship and not an "I-It" relationship. "I-Thou" relations in and of themselves are "mutual, reciprocal, symmetrical, and contentless."[9] Or as Catherine LaCugna suggests, "God is personal because God is relational.... God's being is fecund, intrinsically dynamic, and therefore intrinsically relational."[10] And Jurgen Moltmann offers, "By virtue of their eternal love, the divine persons exist so intimately with one another, for one another, and in one another that they constitute themselves in their unique, incomparable, and complete unity.... The three persons form their unity by themselves in the circulation of the divine life."[11]

Human beings, as God's image bearers, exist for and in relationships—freedom-producing, life-giving relationships—with God and others. "The community of Father, Son, and Spirit becomes the prototype of the human community dreamed of by those who wish to improve society and build it in such a way as to make it into the image and likeness of the Trinity."[12]

In applying this trinitarian perspective, flourishing organizations and people experience the joy, beauty and challenge—as well as the messiness—of being in relationship, of being in community. Each person's identity and gifts are cherished while at the same time commitment to shared purposes fully unites. Each is able to experience the security of belonging, the dignity of contribution and the respect of authentic communication, even in difficult times. The concept of flourishing assumes connection and reciprocity.

THE NEUROSCIENCE OF CONNECTION

The imprint of the Trinity is even found in us physically. New discoveries in neuroscience reveal that our brains function well only when we are connected, in relationship with others.

This should be no surprise. In fact, our brains primarily develop through relationships. In utero and from the time we are born, consistent, present relationships, especially with primary caregivers, form the neural connections our brains need for healthy development and ongoing transformation. Due to mirroring neurons in the brain, we are predisposed to imitate those close to us. "To flourish and to mature into persons of wisdom and Christian virtue, we need the shaping that comes with the best sorts of human relationships."[13]

Connection with others happens in the part of the brain called the limbic system, which is considered the emotional part of the brain. The amygdala, which triggers our flight-or-fight response, is part of the limbic system. Interestingly, the limbic system is an "open-loop" system that relies on external "connections with other people for our own emotional stability."[14] In fact, "one person transmits signals that can alter hormone levels, cardiovascular function, sleep rhythms, and even immune function inside the body of another. Open-loop design means that other people can change our very physiology—and so our emotions."[15]

In other words, the limbic system needs connection and interaction to function healthily. In its natural state of interaction, it observes the emotions of those it encounters and communicates this information to other parts of the brain for processing. Thus, in the organizational context, the limbic system of each person constantly scans and communicates, whether or not the person is conscious of this process. Because of this interconnectedness, one's emotions profoundly affect the emotions of another, especially if he or she happens to be a leader.

Overwhelming scientific evidence suggests that "certain things leaders do—specifically, exhibit empathy and become attuned to others' moods—literally affect both their own brain chemistry and that of their followers."[16] The leader-follower dynamic is a system of conscious and subconscious interaction. Therefore, the leader, educator, facilitator, administrator or pastor profoundly affects whether people thrive or wilt in any given organization.[17]

Synthesizing the latest research in neurobiology, Daniel Goleman and his team present the rationale for this dynamic.[18] People flourish and become their best in environments where there is "resonance—when leaders drive emotions positively."[19] Likewise, there is "dissonance—when leaders drive emotions negatively, undermining the emotional foundations that let people shine."[20] This is due to our limbic systems.

Earlier I mentioned this definition of flourishing from Barbara Fredrickson and Marcial Losada: "to live within an optimal range of human functioning, one that connotes goodness, generativity, growth, and resilience," while "languishing [refers to] people who describe their lives as 'hollow' or 'empty.'"[21] Based on what we've seen about neuroscience, then, leaders are instrumental in helping organizations and the people in them to flourish. They inspire creativity, experimentation and growth. This is because human beings, due to the mirroring neurons in our brains, have a tendency to take on what their limbic systems sense in another person. "Feeling good lubricates mental efficiency, making people better at understanding information ... as well as more flexible in their thinking ... more optimistic about their ability to achieve a goal, enhance creativity."[22]

RELATIONSHIPS IN FLOURISHING ORGANIZATIONS

This reality offers profound potential and possibilities for influence on people and the world. People thrive and are transformed in contexts where there is meaningful connection. This is the image of God in us. Flourishing organizational environments stimulate trusting, freedom-producing relationships. Knowledge and information are shared. Communication is open and transparent. Individuals sense belonging through welcoming on boarding, orientation procedures and training. They understand how their work contributes to the overall mission.

Increasingly, friendships develop; freedom stimulates experimentation; collaboration encourages creative and effective strategies; ongoing learning increases effectiveness.

In chapter nine I explore the concept of organizational culture and particularly note Edgar Schein's research connecting the importance of leadership in the formation of organizational culture.[23] Recent findings in neuroscience validate Schein's conclusion and explain how it relates to the anatomy and physiology of the brain. Individuals tend to key into the leaders, whether positional or not. What leaders feel, model and pay attention to directly impacts others in the organization whether they realize it or not. Leaders stimulate thriving.

Stop and Think

Take a minute to jot down your thoughts on these questions:
- Generally, what's your mood at work?
- Are you satisfied with your job or not? How do you express that verbally or with nonverbal cues?
- What effect do you think your attitudes have on your coworkers?

Obviously, people do not always have positive emotions, making it difficult to create resonance. This is where Goleman's other domains of emotional intelligence (EI) come into play. The most effective leaders are emotionally intelligent. Beyond technical and cognitive competencies, the domains of EI are the most important for successful leading.[24]

Emotional intelligence comprises four domains. The first is self-awareness, which consists of recognizing one's emotions and their impact on others. It means knowing one's strengths and limitations. Self-awareness enables people to stay in touch with their feelings and how they impact others. The second domain of emotional intelligence is self-management. This includes self-control, adaptability and transparency, which means being open about one's feelings. When we share about ourselves wisely, this increases trust.[25] Third is social awareness involving empathy toward and awareness of the emotions of others. Fourth is relationship management, which includes inspiration, bonding, teamwork, conflict resolution and developing others.[26]

Since the patterns of our brains aren't fixed, over time we can form new patterns with new habits and new stimuli. Due to the flexibility, or neuroplasticity, of the brain, people can increase their emotional intelligence.

Jack was startled to hear his staff team thought he hated them. When Richard, my colleague, interviewed the team in order to develop an executive coaching plan for Jack, they shared that when Jack entered the office each morning, he walked past everyone without saying a word and closed his office door. Used to their previous director who liked to "chit chat," they assumed that Jack was unhappy with them and feared he may lay them off in order to bring in his own team. During the interview, Richard discovered high levels of anxiety and fear that impacted their work, making them even more fearful of losing their jobs.

When Richard discussed the staff team's fears with Jack, he was completely shocked. Not only did Jack like the team, he was satisfied with their work, and he was clueless as to why they would feel otherwise. Richard shared how they perceived Jack's posture when he arrived in the mornings. Again, Jack was flabbergasted. He walked straight to his office and closed the door because he was excited about his work but overwhelmed with the amount to do. He had no idea how this was impacting the staff team.

Stop and Think

Here are some questions you might ask about your organization to begin to evaluate how well relationships are flourishing or not:

- How would you describe connection and relationships in your organization? Consistently deepening? Stratified according to hierarchy?
- How readily transparent are leaders and individuals? Are meetings "closed door," secret?

> - Who really knows what is going on in the organization? Everyone? A handful of leaders?
> - Is there laughter? Humor? Are people silent or vocal in meetings? Is there freedom to question, offer suggestions, try new ideas?

Richard and Jack, as part of Jack's coaching, devised a plan for Jack to stop and greet each person as he came in each morning. They also decided he would institute a tea break to encourage informal talks and "checking in." The atmosphere in the office improved immensely and eventually the tea breaks became a normal part of the office's daily activities. Jack became more cognizant of individuals' demeanors and when they were doing well and when they weren't. These new habits changed Jack as well. The rhythm and connection with others decreased his stress.

Because we're created in God's image—the Triune God, three persons united in one—we flourish when we connect, when we experience deep relationships. Our very physiology supports connection. Likewise, God's image in us unites us to his mission, to which we now turn.

INTERDEPENDENCE IN MISSION

We've explored God's image in us as the Trinity—the unity and connection of persons. The Trinity also provides another insight for flourishing organizations. God as Trinity models mutuality and submission—the offering and receiving of each person's role in a united mission. Trinitarian theology highlights the participative process of God's purposes in the world and our partnership in God's redemptive mission. The Gospels disclose "three persons at work rather than one."[27] "All three 'depend' on each other in the dynamic process of the shifting of the kingdom from one divine person to the other."[28]

In time and space, the activity and relationship of the three moves from one to another. The Father entrusts redemptive purposes to the Incarnate Son. At the same time, the Son submits to the Father's will and receives empowerment from the Spirit. The Father and Son entrust the manifestation of the kingdom to the Spirit (and to humans!) until the new heaven and new earth when all will see God's goodness.[29] In other words, in the divine activity, all persons in the Trinity surrender and submit to the work of the other two.

Colin Gunton states it this way: "God is no more than what Father, Son, and Spirit give to and receive from each other in the inseparable communion that is the outcome of their love.... There is no 'being' of God other than this dynamic of persons in relation."[30] If the divine persons in the Trinity mutually participate together in unity, trusting one another in their roles, how much more should our organizations invite the participation of each person in meaningful contribution? The Trinity models what a flourishing organization could be—where each person's identity and dignity is cherished while at the same time the fellowship of purpose fully unites.

MUTUAL PARTICIPATION

Theologians propose that because of the relationships in the Trinity and because humans are created in God's image, human relationships should likewise be mutual, reciprocal and egalitarian. Healthy relationships assume reciprocity. People offer themselves and receive others in the context of accomplishing the organization's or team's vision. Each contributes unique gifts, talents and experiences in an environment that delights in the contribution of one another (Rom 12:3-8). Mirsalov Volf proposes that the Holy Spirit encourages responsibility and interdependence among people, leading to the creation of open, participative structures over against "isolationist" tendencies in organizations.[31]

Remember Adam, the Herman Miller factory worker? Max De Pree and the other leaders of Herman Miller created an open, participative environment, where every person, no matter their role, contributes to the good of the whole company. Designers, factory workers, engineers, managers, secretaries, board members and janitors offer their unique perspectives, experiences and gifts, which synergize to generate a better company. In fact, organizational leaders trust products of this participative process so much, all employees share in the profits of the company each year.

The Trinity is a divine paradigm or model for the relationships of leaders and individuals in organizations. The practical implications of this paradigm are that relationships "should never be authoritarian, coercive or dictatorial. Love, and service, not command and control, characterize relations within the life of the Godhead."[32] This paradigm also informs the navigation between "top down" (hierarchical) and "leaderless team" (egalitarian) dynamics. In the leader-follower relationship, the leader needs to reconcile these apparent opposites regarding the structure of decision making and communication.

AGENCY AND POWER

At the beginning of this chapter we mentioned the founder of Africa Future. We don't know all the factors that caused his lack of trust in Africans. Perhaps it was past or current experiences. Perhaps it was a sense of superiority. As already stated, we can deduce, however, his faith assumptions regarding human agency, power and control. They might go something like this: "Humans are inherently bad. When given the opportunity, workers will take advantage of the organization and therefore must be controlled with strict regulations and policies. Rules and regulations are the best antidote for corruption." We all have faith assumptions regarding people and power. Here is where an orthodox, robust understanding of God's existence as Trinity has potential to shape foundational values for a flourishing organization.

Father, Son and Spirit exist in love and unite in mission. All participate in creation and each intervenes to redeem men and women from corruption and death. The Father trusts the Son to act, who "emptied himself, taking the form of a slave, being born in human likeness" (Phil 2:7), and the Spirit to empower him. At the same time the Father participates by fully communicating with the Son.

> Jesus said to them, "Very truly, I tell you, the Son can do nothing on his own, but only what he sees the Father doing; for whatever the Father does, the Son does likewise. The Father loves the Son and shows him all that he himself is doing; and he will show him greater works than these, so that you will be astonished." (Jn 5:19-20)

Each person in the Trinity participates in dynamic love and invites all humanity into the circle. Throughout history God also entrusts his mission to men and women (Abraham, Sarah, Isaac, Jacob, Moses, Deborah, Samuel, David, Abigail, Esther, Joseph, Mary and so on). After the crucifixion, death and resurrection of Jesus, God empowered all followers of Jesus for his mission. In doing so, the Father and Son also entrust the mission to the Spirit. Jesus said to his disciples, "I have called you friends, because I have made known to you everything that I have heard from my Father" (Jn 15:15).

Interestingly, agency and participation include leadership. In the creation mandate that we have looked at before, men and women are both created in the image and likeness of God "*so that they may rule* over the fish in the sea and the birds in the sky, over the livestock and all the wild animals, and over all the creatures that move along the ground" (Gen 1:26-28 NIV). God's creation blessing includes men and women ruling and acting as wise regents—God-appointed leaders and stewards of creation—for a flourishing creation. Man and woman's eventual disobedience and refusal to be in relationship with God also leads to broken relationships with each other, and the curse establishes hierarchy in their relationship: "Yet your desire shall be for your husband, and he shall rule over you" (Gen 3:16). However, Jesus enters the human dilemma and decisively begins the reverse of the curse until we find, in Revelation 21:1-5, that men and women rule with God once again in the new heaven and the new earth.

In the meantime, God indwells followers of Jesus and offers the power to participate in his redemptive mission. Accountants, data processers, fundraisers, vice presidents, team leaders and janitors are indwelt by the Spirit and play significant roles in all that God is doing. It doesn't matter how much education one has, whether or not someone can read or write, or if they are medical doctors or PhDs. We all participate in the journey back to God's original creation intentions, and our organizations create the context for transformation toward this final eventuality.

MAKING A DIFFERENCE

Students in my organization development classes are often frustrated by what I teach them. They know the problems in their organizations and see how it could be better. Often times, however, they do not occupy significant or "top-level" leadership roles, and so they feel powerless to implement ideas and strategies that could make a difference. How do you "manage up" the ladder?

Remembering how systems thinking works, however, we know we are all connected to the whole organization, no matter how insignificant we might feel. We all participate in the cause-effect loops. We can all have an impact in our particular sphere that makes a difference in the whole, even if we cannot readily see the results. If we do nothing, allowing problems to persist without saying anything, then we are actually contributing to that system as well. We are complicit.

While coaching a team of church planters in the Philippines, my colleague and I noticed significant changes in team dynamics when one team member, Grace, was present. The other members became more quiet, unwilling to offer ideas or contribute. In individual interviews, we asked about this and learned that members feared Grace's anger. On several occasions while discussing strategy, she disagreed with team members so vehemently that one young woman left the team and the others acquiesced. The team now perpetuated a state of polite compliance.

We asked what their best hope was for the future. All team members, except Grace's husband, hoped Grace would leave the team. They felt that if Grace left, they could pursue the mission to which they had been called. Such a solution was, of course, a quick fix. My colleague and I sensed the possibility for a deeper, transformative intervention that would change the lives of everyone on the team and be instructive for their new church. But first we had to gain the commitment of each team member.

We continued sessions with the whole team and privately with each person. With individuals, we asked how their personal behavior contributed to the current team dynamics. Most were surprised by the question and to discover how much they had disconnected from the team. Despite their commitment to the church plant, they didn't want to deal with Grace and the confrontational situations. In their own way, they each told us, "I just want to keep my head down and do my work." They came to realize that their own disconnection actually enabled Grace's behavior and poor team dynamics to continue. They were complicit participants in the dismal situation. We tried to help them envision ways they could authentically re-engage.

During the whole-team sessions, we asked members to revisit their calling and the vision God had given the team. We asked the team what others would see, feel and experience if they completed their God-given vision. How would they know the vision had been accomplished? Excitement built as the team participated in imagining and re-envisioning.

In the next session, each person recounted their own calling and then the team affirmed the gifts they saw in that person. We ended this session with a prayer time of thankfulness for God's calling and the gifts, which naturally segued into a time of recommitment.

During this time, Grace expressed that she knew something was wrong—that she sensed the team's distance from her and her husband. She asked why. Rico took the first brave step. He recalled a team meeting when Grace had expressed her anger and walked out. Rico shared that after that, he had chosen not to offer his ideas and opinions. He asked the team's forgiveness for withholding his contribution. Grace asked if other team members felt the same way as Rico. She painfully observed all, except her husband, nod their heads. "Why didn't you come and talk to me?" Grace asked.

In the end, the team reconciled and reaffirmed their commitment to each other and their mission. They realized God sovereignly led each person—including Grace—to the team in order to contribute his or her unique gifts and be transforming agents for the others and their context. At the same time, they recognized each other's weaknesses and pledged to create safety and protect those areas. Our next step was to help the team create a list of values and a covenant that would guide them forward.

Leaders who understand how the shape and character of the Trinity affects all our relationships are more likely to build trust through an environment that facilitates service, mutuality, community and participation. This is a flourishing organization.

5
DNA: THE LIFE FORCE OF FLOURISHING ORGANIZATIONS

Bill couldn't wait to share the good news. He had just received word that a donor had offered five acres of beautiful, wooded land along with seed money for building a new church campus just outside the city. He would share the news at the elders' meeting that night.

As pastor of the downtown, inner-city church, Bill had struggled with the constant demands of the upkeep of an old building and the flow of immigrants, homeless persons, office workers and loft dwellers. While the church certainly thrived in its current location—many needs were met and people were equipped for ministry—the land and new building would give the church the opportunity to expand. Bill found himself dreaming of state-of-the-art facilities and all that could be built on five acres. He felt the new campus would increase the church's ability to serve and perhaps provide the means for more ministries.

***

Janet, the long-term CEO of a nonprofit ministry, gathered her key staff. They had been struggling financially and weren't sure if they were going to be able to keep their doors open. The lynchpin to the future seemed to be a grant request they had made to a key foundation. Now she had the answer. "The foundation has positively responded! We'll be able to make payroll for another year!"

"They accepted our full proposal?" the team asked.

"Well, not exactly. If we change our mission statement slightly, it will match their criteria for awards, and we will receive the $150,000 grant. But that shouldn't be a problem. After all, it is just a statement, and we don't really refer to it that often anyway. I don't think most people in the organization even know what our mission statement is."

***

The above snapshots represent real situations and well-meaning people in organizations who want to make a difference. Both organizations have arrived at critical junctures where potential quick fixes could jeopardize their ability to flourish.

Crises, whether geopolitical, financial or natural, often reveal and potentially alter the true nature of organizations. How do opportunities for land and new buildings change the ministries of churches? How will moving outside the city alter the purpose of Bill's church? Was Janet right that the mission statement was really just changeable words? What does it mean to alter the "mission" for funding purposes?

***

Henry was new on the job at an inner-city mission that was over a hundred years old, and he had a huge hill to climb. "The board demands that our organization become fiscally solvent in one year's time," he told Phil, his operations officer. "My first mandate as the new president is to address a $600,000 shortfall."

"Wow! One year? Do you know what you'll do?" asked Phil. "Do you have a sense of how, when and where money is received and spent?"

"I haven't a clue," Henry confessed. "The financial director says that it's 'complicated' and not easy to 'display' in simple fashion, especially for nonfinance people. It seems I've inherited a mess."

***

Conversations similar to these, too many to count, pervade board and executive leaders' agendas, especially after an economic downturn. Many well-meaning managers and business consultants wrangle in long meetings to propose plans that keep organizations financially viable, yet potentially compromise the overall purpose and vision—again, quick fixes that put flourishing at risk.

Though critical, Henry's financial crisis as the new president of an older organization is not solely a matter of understanding the inflow of revenue, outflow of expenses and the overall budget. So, when time is short—and the finances must be addressed in a brief timeframe—how can organization leaders make informed decisions that will release energy for flourishing? How can leaders make short-term decisions that won't cripple the long-term mission or purpose of the organization? When crises are urgent, how can leaders ensure long-term sustainability and growth? And more importantly, how can they do so in ways that are authentic to the history and identity of the organization?

At these critical junctures, organization leaders must collectively capture, along with their entire constituency, the essence of the organization: its DNA.[1] For it is only in articulating identity and adapting to the context that organizations may address short-term crises without creating long-term vision drift that could lead to stagnation and, potentially, death. Using an analogy from evolutionary biology, when adapting to the context, the organization must protect the DNA, eliminate elements of the DNA that do not serve the organization's survival, and create new arrangements of DNA that enable the organization to thrive.[2]

Are mission and vision statements just statements? Well, yes and no. A community called together to participate in the mission of God is sacred. And because communities are as unique as individual human beings—history, personality, gifts, culture, calling and so on—their sacredness rests in their identity, their essence. They are to offer a unique contribution in God's kingdom. Therefore, no, a one-sentence statement of mission and vision is not critical, but embracing a unique call to participate in God's mission is absolutely critical. For organizations, this call can be characterized as vision, mission, faith assumptions and values[3]—the DNA, the life force of the organization (see figure 5.1).

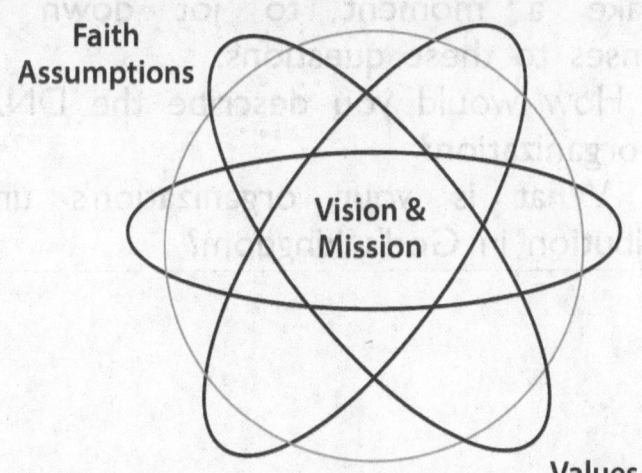

Figure 5.1. The organizational DNA loops

The most well-written vision, mission, faith assumptions and values statements may not capture who an organization truly is. But crises can all too clearly reveal this reality. Perhaps that is why people today experience such fatigue and cynicism as they approach vision and mission statements or processes that capture them. They sense faddish copycats and lack of authenticity. And when push comes to shove in a crisis, leaders often make decisions contrary to the vision and mission, which in the long run threatens the identity and overall purpose of the organization. Mission, vision and values are intricately connected to strategies, structures and polices (see figure 5.2), therefore, they must be at the forefront of any organizational decision.

> **Stop and Think**
> Take a moment to jot down your responses to these questions:
> • How would you describe the DNA of your organization?
> • What is your organization's unique contribution in God's kingdom?

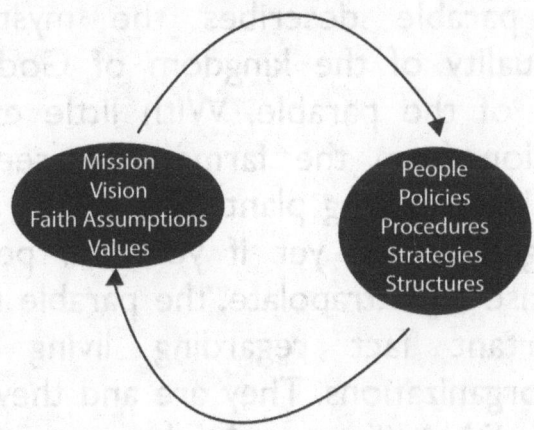

Figure 5.2. Cause-effect loop of DNA in organizations

DNA—VISION, MISSION, FAITH ASSUMPTIONS AND VALUES

Assuming nutritious soil, the seed sprouts, grows and produces grain. It flourishes. As Jesus said,

> The kingdom of God is as if someone would scatter seed on the ground, and would sleep and rise night and day, and the seed would sprout and grow, he does not know how. The earth produces of itself, first the stalk, then the head, then the full grain in the head. But when the grain is ripe, at once he goes in with his sickle, because the harvest has come. (Mk 4:26-29)

Given the right conditions, the seed becomes what it is meant to become—a full head of grain ready for harvest. The seed's DNA directs what it becomes.

This parable describes the mystery and organic quality of the kingdom of God. That is the point of the parable. With little effort and no direction from the farmer, the seed grows into a grain-producing plant. This is not a parable about organizations, yet if you will permit me some license to extrapolate, the parable illustrates an important fact regarding living systems, including organizations. They are and they become what their DNA dictates. At the same time, they are influenced by and respond to the environment they are in (a constant feedback loop)—sometimes adapting and producing more fruit (the results for which they exist), sometimes mutating and becoming something different, and sometimes ceasing to exist.

Extrapolating further, organizations are living systems with unique identities. They are communities of people created to flourish—created for unique living in and contribution to God's kingdom. Identity is passed from one generation to the next. I propose that all communities (organizations, if you like) inherently contain mission, vision, faith assumptions and values, and that is their DNA.[4] Therefore mission, vision, faith assumptions and values are not static in the sense of statements created and forgotten, but rather are replicating, life-giving, purpose-revealing, dynamic-innovating processes that ensure the ongoing growth and adaptive existence of an organization—by definition, flourishing.

The identity of a called community, or its DNA, is best understood in the overlap of mission, vision, faith assumptions and values. What does each of these terms mean?

- *Vision* is the picture of future outcomes and results God has called the organization to accomplish.
- *Mission* is what the community does to accomplish the vision.[5]
- *Faith assumptions* are the community's beliefs—about who God is, who we are and what the nature of the world is like—that influence decisions and actions as they accomplish the vision.
- *Values* are the things we think really matter as an organization, which guide us as we decide what would be right and what would be wrong for us to do.

In this light, mission, vision, faith assumptions and values should definitely *not* be nice statements that leaders write and then put on posters—or more often, file away in a binder on a bookshelf. Rather, mission, vision, faith assumptions and values are the unique life force of organizations to which individuals are called to participate and to which the organization will be held accountable. Therefore, it is absolutely necessary that the mission, vision, faith assumptions and values are articulated, explained, taught and reproduced in the everyday life of the organization. If the organization's DNA is present in each member, there is little need for controlling rules and policies. The life force of the DNA will naturally produce the appropriate fruit.

Vision and mission. In recent years, much has been written to urge congregations, organizations and businesses to write vision and mission statements. Throughout Scripture God uses words to paint a picture of the future—vision—like this:

> For the Lord your God is bringing you into a good land, a land with flowing streams, with springs and underground waters welling up in valleys and hills, a land of wheat and barley, of vines and fig trees and pomegranates, a land of olive trees and honey, a land where you may eat bread without scarcity, where you will lack nothing, a land whose stones are iron and from whose hills you may mine copper. (Deut 8:7-9)

God also invites us to participate in his work—mission—like this: "You shall love the Lord your God with all your heart, and with all your soul, and with all your might" (Deut 6:5).

Often people struggle to distinguish between vision and mission. This is understandable since many use the words interchangeably. Here is an easy way to distinguish between the two. Vision relates to seeing. Simply stated, vision is a God-given, future picture of the results and outcomes of a called community's work.[6] If they accomplish what God is calling them to accomplish, what will it look like? What will the results be? The outcomes? Mission, on the other hand, is what God calls a community to do in order to accomplish the vision. Vision is a faith-filled picture (nouns) of future results. Mission is action, doing (verbs). Table 5.1 shows examples of the difference between vision and mission statements for three well-known nonprofit organizations.

For communities of faith, the overarching biblical mandate is to participate in God's mission, resulting in kingdom-of-God-shaped communities and the future God intends. Yet like every unique human being, congregations and organizations have unique purposes and calls to mission with unique results in the kingdom. The uniqueness comes with the overlap of vision, mission, faith assumptions and values, to which we turn next.

Table 5.1. Examples of vision and mission statements

Organization	Vision Statement (A Picture of the Future)	Mission Statement (What We Do to Accomplish the Vision)
Habitat for Humanity	A world where everyone has a decent place to live.	To put God's love into action, Habitat for Humanity brings people together to build homes, communities and hope.
Kiva	A world where all people—even in the most remote areas of the globe—hold the power to create opportunity for themselves and others.	To connect people through lending to alleviate poverty.
World Vision	For every child, life in all its fullness; our prayer for every heart, the will to make it so.	To follow our Lord and Savior Jesus Christ in working with the poor and oppressed to promote human transformation, seek justice and bear witness to the good news of the kingdom of God.

Faith assumptions and values. Faith assumptions and values are foundational to mission and vision. They are the standards or principles an organization holds to be most important that cause individuals to make decisions to act the way they do. They represent how a community aspires to act or function as it carries out its mission in pursuit of its vision. Remember, faith assumptions and values exist in a cause-effect loop. For example, an organization that has Romans 12:3-8 as a foundational text, highlighting the importance of the body and members of the body contributing their individual gifts, could have the value of "everyone participates." Likewise, in turn, the value "everyone participates" strengthens the faith assumption of Romans 12:3-8.

Values describe what matters most—the kind of people we are, the type of work we do and how we behave as we do the work. Values determine behavior. They undergird every aspect

of ministry. Here are examples of values from various organizations or teams:
- People matter more than programs.
- We practice incarnational ministry.
- We celebrate diversity in unity.
- Networking: We gladly work with others in the body of Christ.
- Pauline sense of urgency: Always work toward multiplication.
- Faith and prayer: We recognize that the ultimate goal is God's glory and that is only accomplished by dependence on him through faith and prayer.
- Perseverance: We recognize that it may take many methods and many failures to finally establish a church-planting movement, and we will not give up but will remain focused on our vision.

Whether articulated or not, every organization has values that determine its decisions, actions and strategies. Actually living out our values increases the likelihood that they, like DNA, will be replicated in future generations.

Getting values in line. Be advised. Values influence our actions *and* our actions also influence our values (a cause-effect loop illustrated in figure 5.3). Organizations will initiate strategy based on values whether or not the values have been articulated. Decisions and actions in line with the stated values strengthen the values.

Decisions and actions not in alignment with values will, over time, change the values.

Christ Community Church, a megachurch located in a Midwestern city of the United States, had a stated value embracing diversity and racial reconciliation. Members wanted the church to represent the ethnicities present in the church's neighborhood—mostly populated by recent immigrants from East Africa and South America—and beyond that, to be a catalyst for racial reconciliation in the city. So they initiated events such as neighborhood BBQs, English and citizenship classes, and preschool to connect with the surrounding neighborhoods. Through these strategies, they expected their neighbors to join the church.

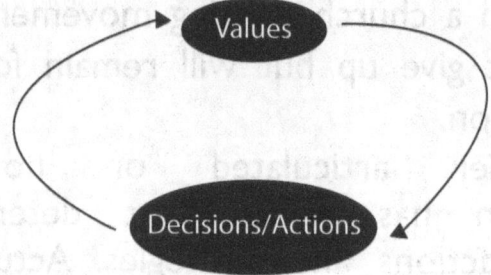

Figure 5.3. The interaction of values and actions

Neighbors did flock to the English and citizenship classes, and because of trust built in these contexts, they even came to the Sunday worship service. In the worship service, however, they felt lost among the two thousand mostly white participants, singing strange music and listening to complex English. The warmth they felt in their classes did not match what they experienced in the worship service. The neighbors felt uncomfortable with the cultural forms of the predominantly white, male leadership. Even the Christian immigrants found they could not join the church.

What was the problem? The events and strategies of the church only minimally demonstrated the expressed value of diversity. True diversity would require deeper commitment and behavioral change. For example, the church would likely need to create a service that was more in tune with the cultural norms of the immigrants. Leaders would also have to find ways to include the immigrants in leadership roles. Finally, the church would need to give these new participants an opportunity to influence other decisions and activities of the church.

Organizations and teams must *behave* their values. It may seem obvious that if a monocultural church is to become diverse, it must change. But often monocultural churches somehow think they can become diverse without changing in significant ways. That was the case with Christ Community Church. Though diversity was a stated value, keeping the status quo was actually a higher (unstated) value. The predominantly white, highly educated congregation enjoyed listening to intellectual sermons and singing hymns. They were comfortable with that, and so resisted deeper change.

How much agreement is necessary for a team to effectively function? Because values influence expectations of behavior, strategy, goals and so on, there must be substantial agreement amongst team members regarding values, even beyond agreement with the mission and vision. In my experience working with teams all over the world, if there is not strong unity around values, the seemingly smallest decisions may consume hours and hours of debate. This is precious kingdom time wasted.

Consider Charmagne's team located in a predominantly Muslim country. Charmagne's organization combined two previously existing teams into one. Their united vision was to see reproducing communities of Jesus followers. When they discussed strategies, however, members of the former two teams differed in their approaches. One faction proposed getting jobs in the community. They highly valued incarnational ministry and therefore concluded that joining the normal life of the community by obtaining jobs would provide opportunities to build relationships and eventually disciple small groups of Jesus followers. The other faction believed locals were the most effective evangelists and disciplers, so they wanted to immediately train locals in church planting and not worry about language learning, living in the community, jobs or other means of connecting.

The members of the team debated strategy during their first team retreat and following team meetings, each faction trying to convince the other of the merits of their strategy. However, due to each person's deeply held values, they were not able to agree on strategy, and therefore the team disbanded.

Finally, values impact morale. Individuals may find a lack of motivation if they sense a widening gap between their personal values and the values of the organization. The same thing can happen if actual organizational practices contradict stated organizational values.

Mark, for example, required his staff team to come on time to meetings. Yet he often arrived fifteen to thirty minutes late himself, always with an apology and the excuse that he was meeting with important officials. The result was not just grumbling among the staff. They began to wonder both how much Mark valued them and their time as well as whether what he said mattered that much. When actions and values don't match, morale plummets.

Values and policies. Policies also need to flow from values. If leaders create policies that undermine the organization's values, unintended consequences can result, including the values themselves changing over time in problematic ways.

Since the beginning of China Inland Mission/OMF International in 1865, J. Hudson Taylor believed in and established a value for sharing resources and decision making regarding strategy happening at the grassroots level (the "field"). Structurally speaking, this meant that the organization pooled the resources. Funds from all over the world came into an account—first in China and then, after expulsion from China, in Singapore—and were then distributed to individual missionaries. Everyone evenly shared what came in and all workers received the same allowances (with local cost-of-living adjustments), whether new to the field or the general director/president.

Pooling resources worked fine when the organization was small and located in one country, but one-hundred-plus years later, functionally speaking, this meant that organizational leaders in Singapore made key decisions that determined who got how much money, what types of schools children could attend (an international school in a large city would require more of the "pool" than an OMF-run boarding school), and so on. Policy decisions regarding money became so complex and arduous that something had to change. Centralized decision making regarding finances also meant that at times it was organizational leaders, predominantly in Singapore, who de facto were the ones devising strategy rather than the field leaders—which was not in line with Taylor's lasting value of field-created and implemented strategies.

The general director commissioned and led a task force to devise a way to decrease centralized finances, increase field and individual decision making regarding the use of finances, and increase personal responsibility for support raising. They faced strong opposition from some. The pooling method had, over the years, become *the* value instead of sharing resources. The task force insightfully realized that they needed to demonstrate how the new policies would actually fulfill OMF's cardinal values of sharing and leadership from local ministry contexts better than the pooling method.

The new financial system pushed finances and finance decision making to the leadership teams in each country. In addition, individuals and families, while maintaining the same standard of living as other OMFers in their context, could create individual budgets to raise money for special expenses, including ministry expenses (such as training, computers and cars), medical expenses and their children's schooling. In this way, these needs would not have to take a larger portion of the "pool." At the same time, each country would decide how to share resources and costs. For example, rental costs may be shared by a team, which works effectively when some housing is offered for free and other housing is expensive. While the new financial system was complex, it enabled OMF to have integrity with their values, while at the same time increasing individual responsibility and choice without negatively impacting the whole organization.

Once the system and technology for supporting the system were in place, the task force and leaders blitzed the organization with all types of media (papers, emails and curriculum), and the general director traveled to all centers in order to communicate and train for the change. Key to this communication was highlighting OMF's time-honored values and demonstrating how the new system enabled increased fulfillment of the values.

CHANGE AND CRISIS

As the story of OMF suggests, values influence policies, yet over time, policies may become values in and of themselves. Over time the original value can be lost because of the ongoing focus on the policy. It's possible though that a value may have so radically changed through time that it is no longer a reference point for the organization. No matter what values have been agreed on or written in the charter documents of organizations, crises may reveal the transformation. That's what happened to Focus on Unreached Peoples (FUP) when the mission redeployed personnel after a civil war to safe countries.

Despite FUP's founding vision to see unreached peoples connect with Jesus and their initial value for risk taking, the leaders made a crisis-based decision to permanently redeploy missionaries to less dangerous, already-churched countries. When redeployment didn't occur back to countries where other unreached peoples were located, it signaled that its values had changed.

Why didn't FUP's leaders recognize this? Perhaps the aging of the organization had something to do with it. Recent college graduates may be more inclined to stay in tumultuous situations than families with young children. Or perhaps the board required an evacuation policy in order to protect itself from liability. No matter what the reason, value-shifting forces were at work, which, in the end, led to vision drift and the long-term demise of the organization.

6

PUTTING YOUR DNA TO WORK

How can a community of faith discern their God-given calling and envision the resulting future? And who does it? Does a leader or leadership team "go to the mountain," receive the vision from God, return and announce it? Or should it be a whole-community process? The following case studies and principles offer varied, tested methods for discerning and articulating vision, mission and values.

CASE 1—FRIENDS IN BERKELEY

A group of friends graduating from the University of California at Berkeley decided they would form a covenant group and meet every year for accountability, prayer and discernment. They put their values down on paper and asked the Lord if he would call them into mission together. Eventually he did. Fourteen years had passed, and the covenant group felt led to start a church in Berkeley and proceeded, based on their values, to dream of and picture the future (vision) as well as what they would do (mission) in their community. Along the way, others were attracted to the values, mission and vision, and joined the church.

CASE 2—ANNA AND HER VILLAGE

Anna returned to her village after attending university in the city. In the early days after her return, she felt overwhelmed by the contrast between her university life and the poverty and needs of her village. Many had been infected with HIV/AIDS, and most families had lost at least one member to the disease. Anna said they could stop the spread of HIV/AIDS and everyone could live productive lives, but the villagers laughed at her. Few could remember a time without the disease. Anna proceeded to envision a future without HIV/AIDS and together with her family and friends created an educational program and developed practices that decreased HIV/AIDS by 50 percent in their village.

CASE 3—THE JUNCTION ARTICULATES ITS VISION

The Junction (now Mercy Town), a church in Southern California, was five years old. Approximately one hundred and fifty members were involved on a weekly basis, yet the leadership team sensed a lack of cohesion and purpose. What were they trying to accomplish?

How could they incorporate a vision beyond running programs and meeting the needs of consumerist culture?

In conjunction with an external consultant, the leaders planned a process—which included every member—to capture and articulate the values and mission of the church. A whole day was set aside for this. Leading up to the day, members were asked to prayerfully respond to three questions: (1) Why did you come to the Junction? (2) Why did you stay? (3) What is one thing you sense God has called the Junction to do but we are not currently doing?

The members were divided into groups of twenty. The day began at 8:00a.m. with each group spending two hours in discussion. Every member had the chance to offer their answers to the three questions, and the consultant captured their responses in a few phrases that she put on sheets of paper and then stuck to a wall. As a group, with the consultant facilitating, the phrases were categorized and prioritized. Interestingly, all groups prioritized the same five categories for why they had come to the Junction and why they had stayed.

From these, the leadership team wrote six values and fed them back to the community in order to check that they had accurately captured the sharing from the day-long event. Some adjustments were made and then re-presented. Also, for the third question, all groups prioritized one thing. From this and other conversations, the leadership team was able to write a mission statement and eventually, a vision statement.

CASE 4—OMF RECAPTURES ITS VISION

A task force consisting of the leadership team and diverse (age, ethnicity, education) members of OMF International (US) met together for three days to begin the process of recapturing the OMF US vision. Leading up to the event, participants were asked to prepare in three ways. First, to prayerfully answer these questions: Why did you join OMF? Why have you stayed with OMF? What are some past and recent compelling stories that indicate God's work in and through OMF? Second, they were asked to research and prepare a three-minute presentation on global trends they believed would bring radical opportunities for OMF and impact its future. Third, all were asked to read notes related to vision, mission and values as well as a SWOT analysis conducted by OMF International.[1]

Meanwhile, the national director communicated with the US membership worldwide to keep them abreast of developments and ask for prayer. During the three-day event, participants shared their research and reflections. Based in this collaborative environment, a facilitator helped the group capture vision, mission and values. Eventually, these results were fed back to the US membership, who were asked for input. Adjustments were made to the mission, vision and values and then finalized for everyone to adopt.

PRINCIPLES FOR DISCERNING AND ARTICULATING VISION, MISSION, FAITH ASSUMPTIONS AND VALUES

These four case studies in capturing vision, mission, faith assumptions and values illustrate three principles:

1. Be as participative as possible. People are naturally drawn together into community to accomplish certain purposes. In other words, because they are a community, they can trust that the Spirit has drawn them together and that stating vision, mission, faith assumptions and values will draw out what is already present. It is a unifying activity. Ultimately, specifying the vision, mission, faith assumptions and values is a way to identify the community DNA, its essence. Being explicit in writing ensures that the DNA is clear and therefore more readily passed on to future generations.

In the first three case studies, most everyone in the communities was involved in the process. But sometimes that is just not possible, such as was the case with OMF, who has a very large staff flung all over the globe. In those cases, developing an extensive and intensive communication program is essential. Doing that is what made OMF's experience so successful.

2. *Adapt the process depending on the age and stage of the organization.* A small group of people dreaming about the future (case 1) is very different than a large organization that must articulate and reclarify vision because it either has drifted or stopped producing the results for which it exists (case 4). The difference in questions may be stated as, Does God want us to do something together? What will the result be? versus, How can we recapture, embrace and be obedient to what God has called us to do? For the church or organization that has lost its kingdom vision, there will need to be preparation (for example, biblical teaching, remembering foundational history, reimagining the future, and possibly, repentance) and participation before articulation.

Many organizations and companies begin with a vision born out of the relationship of the founders. Hewlett-Packard began when two recent engineering graduates, Bill Hewlett and Dave Packard, decided they wanted to start a company. Only then did they start experimenting with things the company might make. In such cases, the DNA may not be articulated until after the initial startup, once the organization is producing the results for which it exists.[2] But it needs to be articulated eventually—and usually sooner rather than later.

3. Connect the DNA to actions and practices. As the DNA (vision, mission, faith assumptions and values) is stated and written down, behaviors, strategies and policies must be aligned with it. More than that, such actions and practices must be in a continuous, reinforcing feedback loop with the DNA. Disconnect between these aspects of organization development results in drift; the organization becomes what it is not meant to be and most often does not produce results in line with God's intentions for that community.

When people own the vision, mission, faith assumptions and values of an organization, when its DNA is replicated over time, they automatically do and become what is intended. There is less need for control, for programs or leadership to make it happen. While following the cues of DNA coding is natural for living organisms, ensuring and replicating the DNA in an organizational context requires vigilance. Following are practices that, if enacted, may serve your contexts.

MAKING YOUR DNA VISIBLE

People need to authentically sense an organization's DNA in their first encounter, whether through a website, social media, graphic materials, people or at events. If being international is a core part of an organization's identity, its website, social media and promotional materials should reveal pictures of their worldwide constituency.

Hiring. When people begin an application and interview process to join an organization, they should also quickly encounter core aspects of its DNA. This can be found in written materials but also in the way they interact with those doing the hiring.

Human resource personnel can also include application questions that, at least on paper, reveal the candidates' faith assumptions and values. For example:
- Share the story of your faith journey and calling to a ministry such as ours.
- Think back to a time when you truly experienced life and energy in your work. Share that story and identify the factors that made the work life giving.

Interview questions can also get at the potential fit a candidate has with the organization's values. Here are some examples:
- Describe the work environment in which you've been the most satisfied and productive.
- What work environment has been the least satisfying for you and why?
- Describe the best boss you've had. What made that person so good?

- Describe tasks you've had in which you worked as part of a team and in which you worked on your own.
- If you could allocate how much time you worked in a team and how much independently, how would you divide your time and why?

If an organization values independent work, then interviewers should be cautious about hiring those who want to work in teams most of the time—even if the candidate is otherwise highly qualified. Likewise, if the best boss a potential employee describes is very different from typical managers in the organization, caution is again needed.

If the organization's culture is transparent and has an expectation for direct communication, interviewers can ask the following:
- Tell us about a time when you experienced conflict with someone in your work setting. How did you know there was conflict? What did you do or not do to resolve the conflict?
- Tell us about a time when you observed someone you supervised needing to improve his or her work. How did you handle this situation? What was the result?

Remember, the application and interview process is a two-way street. If you are applying for a job, you can probe its mission, vision, faith

assumptions and values by asking questions such as,
- Tell me about a recent decision regarding ministry strategies when there were real options. How did you choose the strategy?
- Share with me how you evaluate each year whether the organization progresses toward the vision. How do you know or not know?

Potential employees can also learn about an organization's DNA by participating in certain events that are core to its identity. For a church, potential members usually go to worship services, retreats or outreach events for some time before deciding to join. Other organizations may also have various public events that prospective employees could participate in or observe.

Ensuring that the vision, mission and values are at the center of the hiring process prevents conflict and heartache. That way, both the organizational leaders and individuals can discern "fit," either connect or disconnect with the DNA.

Orientation and training. After hiring comes orientation and training. What is key to your organization? Creativity, efficiency, relationships, teamwork, family, financial responsibility, sales, technology or growth? Whatever it is, these should be emphasized not just verbally or in writing but in the way the orientation and training actually takes place. If your organization values teamwork, orientation should not be largely a one-on-one affair. If it values creativity, training had better not be boring.

Suppose the mission of Global Christian Partners (GCP) is "to create and support indigenous, church-planting movements." Because developing indigenous leadership is at the core, missionaries joining GCP may never preach a sermon or baptize in the host country since doing so may hinder the formation of local leadership. Rather, they will likely coach existing leaders to preach and baptize. Similarly, say a central value of In Touch (IT), a campus ministry, is working in teams. You wouldn't expect IT to send an individual to begin pioneering work on a new campus without a team if they desire to stay true to this value.

DNA in daily activities. Ultimately the vision, mission, faith assumptions and values can translate into daily activities in two ways: first, by ensuring the flow from the mission and vision to goals and action plans; second, by connecting evaluation, planning and budgeting processes to the mission and vision as well (see figure 6.1).

Strategies, informed and constrained by the organization's core values and faith assumptions, flow from the vision and mission. Translating strategies into reality requires the creation of goals, preferably SMARTER goals—specific, measurable, achievable, relevant, time oriented, evaluated and reviewed goals (see table 6.1). Such goals lead to activities that accomplish the action plans (who will do what by when and with what resources). SMARTER goal setting is comprehensive and, if practiced, helps you move toward the vision and mission.

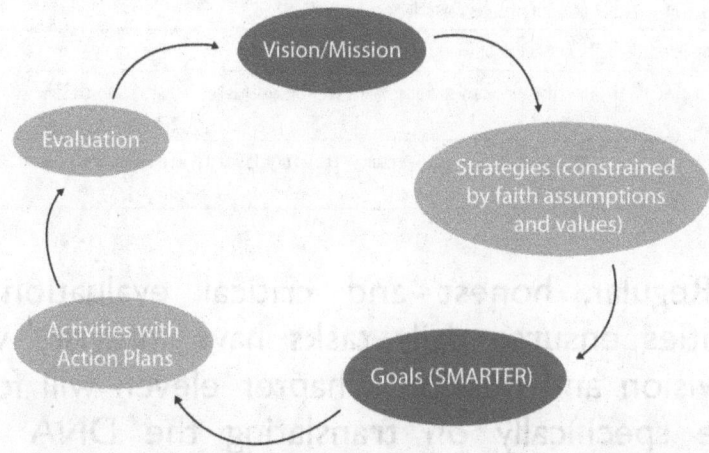

Figure 6.1. Building DNA into daily activities

For a church-planting team with a vision for multiplying churches through small groups (strategy), here are two SMARTER goals:
1. Invite and train twelve new small group leaders by December 31. Evaluate progress toward this goal in our biweekly team meeting and review on December 31.
2. Based on the Sunday worship service theme, write integrating curriculum for the small groups by October 31. The first draft for evaluation and feedback will be due September 30. Review and amend strategy toward the goal as needed during team meetings.

Table 6.1. SMARTER goals

Specific	The explicit target of the goal
Measurable	A numeric expression of what will be seen when the goal is reached
Achievable	A realistic goal for the context and time frame
Relevant	A goal that advances the strategy
Time Oriented	The specific date by which the goal will be accomplished
Evaluated	A goal that will be assessed afterward to see if the goal has been accomplished or not and why or why not
Reviewed	After evaluation, new or revised goals will be set to help you stay on track in working toward the strategy

Regular, honest and critical evaluation of activities ensures daily tasks have integrity with the vision and mission. Chapter eleven will focus more specifically on translating the DNA into daily realities.

Often budgeting processes have little linkage to the vision, mission, faith assumptions and values. Especially in complex multinational or multidepartmental organizations, the yearly budgeting cycle references and builds on the previous year, and compiling the budget can become so arduous, most organizational leaders are just relieved to have a budget in place before the next fiscal year begins. Yet if the planning and budgeting process proceeds without asking, Did our activities and stewardship of resources bring us closer to the vision this year? or, Did we spend money in alignment with our mission and values? then it is likely that over time the planning, budgeting cycle will become completely disconnected from the vision, mission, faith assumptions and values of the organization. This could lead to the potentially dangerous reality of the organization existing just for the sake of existence and not for a compelling purpose and future. Therefore, as time consuming as the process may seem, leaders and budget managers must first evaluate (checking for alignment with the vision, mission and values), then plan (according to the vision, mission and values) and finally set the budget.

> ### Stop and Think
> Take a moment now to reflect on your organization's budgeting process.
> - Who does the budgeting?
> - When does it begin?
> - What happens before it begins?
> - What are the procedures?
> - Who approves the budget?

Senior leaders from Agape start their budgeting process on a retreat each year. One leader facilitates the weekend by first leading a prayer time, during which they ask the Holy Spirit to reveal the ways Agape advanced toward their vision in the past year. The leaders fill the walls of the retreat center with flip-chart papers of stories and illustrations that capture movement toward the vision. Then the leaders pause to celebrate and thank God for his goodness and unfailing love through a special dinner.

The next day, one of the leaders facilitates a silent retreat, asking everyone to reflect, pray and listen to God for pictures and/or words that encapsulate God's leading and desired interventions for the upcoming year. After gathering each leader's impressions, the team notices and draws out themes, which then provide the basis for planning and goals. The leaders only begin the budgeting process after the weekend retreat. They've found through the years that their individual notions of what the budget should be often change once they review the previous year and pause to listen to God and each other. They sense that this discipline enables them to stay vision driven rather than money driven. Figure 6.2 captures the order of their budgeting process.

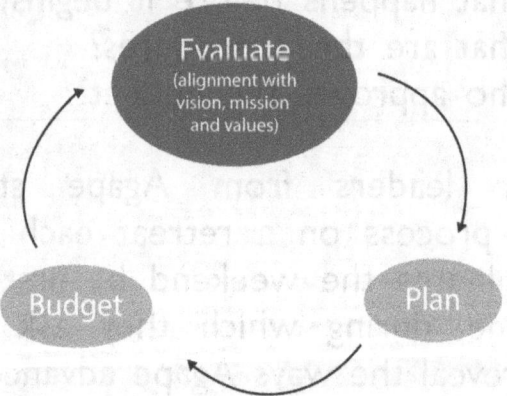

Figure 6.2. Aligning your budget with your DNA

PUTTING DNA TO WORK IN THE BOARD

Ideally, you can find the DNA of an organization or church in each member. Minimal external controls or rules are then needed because the vision, mission, faith assumptions and values naturally live, produce fruit and reproduce through each person. This is flourishing. However, normally churches and organizations should have a group whose responsibility is to regularly research and evaluate whether or not the community is staying true to its purpose. These groups (board of directors, elders, council or the like) are responsible to confirm or correct the work of the organization.

Normally boards receive reports from the CEO or other leaders in the organization. I recommend that such reports always connect with the mission and vision so that everyone is clear why they do what they do and accomplish what they accomplish. This is a needed, ongoing organizational discipline.

Mission and vision are most in danger during a crisis, whether one of finances, internal conflict or an unexpected leadership transition. That's what happened with FUP in chapter one.

Crises also present new opportunities for creativity and pursuing the vision in more radical and effective ways. The board's contribution and presence during crises leads to mission drift or mission integrity.

Consider this case. Before Joseph began his tenure as the CEO of the Barnabas Foundation, the organization drew down on its principle year after year. The board saw that if this practice continued, the doors of the foundation would close in ten years. When Joseph began, he relied on his financial experience from the private sector to create policies that ensured the longevity and sustainability of the foundation, while maintaining generous giving to worthy proposals. He then reorganized the foundation's financial investments to bring greater return. Joseph and the board chair worked together and facilitated a process to clarify the mission and vision of the foundation. As a result of four years of tireless efforts, not only was the organization on more solid financial footing but grants were now consistently being awarded on criteria based on their DNA.

Then Joseph's eight-year-old daughter contracted a rare form of leukemia. Despite the fruitful turnaround, Joseph now felt he must step down in order to care for his daughter.

The board supported Joseph's decision and immediately accepted his resignation. Now they had to deal with the crisis of this leadership vacuum just when the organization was on track. Several board members recommended a CEO with similar expertise and experience as Joseph's. Joseph's work was outstanding. Why not choose someone with the same skill set? Others recommended they promote from within the foundation and appoint one of the directors.

Rather than appoint someone quickly (a potential quick fix)—even though the CEO's absence could negatively impact the organization—the board chose to slow down, study the current state of the foundation and compile the characteristics and qualifications of the next CEO based on their study. In the meantime, the board chair stepped in to provide overall leadership for the foundation, since she was retired and had the freedom to do so.

The results of the study surprised the board members. They found that while Joseph's contribution set the foundation on the right track, this was not the skill set required for the next era of the organization. Rather, as the board revisited the mission and vision, the heart of which centered on serving organizations to build their capacity, it became clear that they needed a leader with experience in and vision for capacity development.

They therefore promoted Michelle, who was one of Barnabas Foundation's directors. Michelle, besides being a strategic leader, had designed and implemented effective leader and organization development initiatives in several international organizations. She lived and breathed capacity development. The foundation's leadership crisis, rather than detracting or causing mission drift, became an opportunity to propel the mission and vision forward into increased focus and effectiveness.

> ### Stop and Think
> Reflect on a significant crisis that has occurred in your organization's history. How did God transform the crisis?
>
> As you review the story, see if you can identify ways the crisis became an opportunity for increased focus on or effectiveness toward the vision.

Effective organizational leadership is not about manipulating statements in order to obtain resources or respond to the latest fad—quick fixes. Rather, excellent leadership happens when, despite crises, decisions and subsequent actions reflect, with integrity, the DNA of the organization. The organization, and the people who comprise it, become what they are meant to be. They flourish and participate in the flourishing kingdom of God.

7

THE DISCIPLINE OF FLOURISHING—ORGANIZATION AND CAPACITY DEVELOPMENT

Alan boarded the plane for his third trip to China in less than a year. Two leadership teams for China Advance Partners (CAP) needed his arbitration for the third time. The two groups just could not work through their differences on strategy and ministry activities.

During his first trip to arbitrate, Alan facilitated discussion and reconciliation between the two teams that led to a compromise everyone agreed to. The teams decided to divide their target region into two, with one team focusing on ministry in western China and the other focusing on eastern China. That solution worked until the Sichuan earthquake. Because of relationships with the Chinese and the medical expertise on both teams, both engaged in relief in Sichuan, and their philosophies clashed again. One valued working only in relationship with and expressed permission from the government, while the other was more entrepreneurial, proceeding ahead when there was opportunity.

The solution arrived at during Alan's second trip seemed straightforward. The CAP teams would complete their relief work after the earthquake, and then one team would continue their focus on trauma counseling, development projects and construction in western China, while the other team continued their church ministry in eastern China. But this plan also failed, because during the earthquake crisis, several new churches had formed and the East China team, which had relationships with the new Chinese pastors, wanted to stay and support their ministries with leader development training. The teams clashed again.

Perhaps, Alan thought as the plane took off, the compromises and agreements weren't working because they only addressed symptoms but not the deeper issues of the teams and CAP's strategies.

***

ZZZ International formed an agency in the 1980s to connect and place Christian academics in universities throughout India. Called Partners with India, the agency grew on the basis of the strong reputation of the professors. Given this success, ZZZ International formed another organization, Medical Partners, in the 1990s to place Christian doctors and dentists in hospitals and universities of India. Meanwhile, Partners with India continued to grow by connecting engineers and other development-type workers with rural projects such as well drilling, reforesting, agricultural, health and literacy programs.

In the 2000s, another group in ZZZ International started a new ministry for church planting amongst unreached people groups of India, predominantly in the North. At the same time, another team began work in northeast India among Indian pastors, developing training curriculum for missions and leadership.

All four branches grew until three hundred ZZZ International members lived in India. Eventually these branches became individual organizations under the umbrella of ZZZ International, each with different mission, vision and values, and administrative, finance, mobilization and training processes. For example, one organization combined their resources and shared them equally among the employees while another structured their finances toward individual family needs and budgets.

This seemed to work fine until the mobilizing personnel in the four organizations competed to recruit members to their own organizations and did not inform potential workers of opportunities in other parts of India with ZZZ International. Over time, the visions of each of the four organizations drifted from the overall vision of ZZZ International.

***

An organization can take people seriously and have well-integrated mission, vision and values—and still have problems. Like any healthy organism, it can have growing pains. Integrating new ideas and changes in its environment can cause bumps in the road. CAP and ZZZ International were facing very typical kinds of problems. Both groups, however, gave in to the temptation to employ quick fixes, which were like putting bandages over wounds that need more serious attention. The result was an infection instead of proper healing.

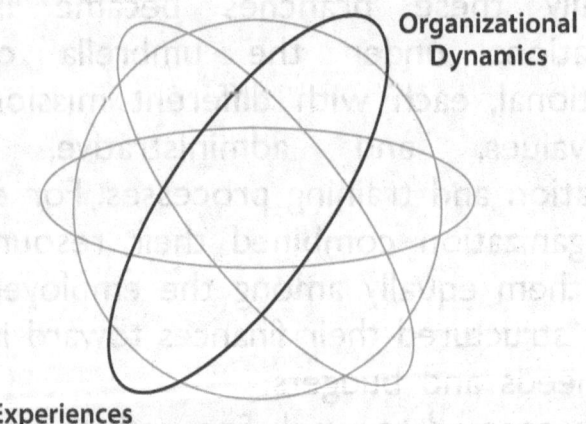

Figure 7.1. The organization action loop

Both CAP and ZZZ were operating primarily in the organization action loop (see figure 7.1) of structure, policies and procedures. Leaders too often make decisions to pursue opportunities or intervene in problematic situations without data and thought directed toward long-term repercussions (cause-effect loops projected into the future). For an organization to flourish, however, more disciplined and structured evaluation is needed. Why? For CAP it was because the solutions applied in the conflicts did not work and the clashes reoccurred. For ZZZ International it was due to the compartmentalization of the four divisions, which caused competition and duplicate administration and structures, and drained resources. For a flourishing organization, leaders must prevent the cycle of reaction to symptoms and unwieldly, inefficient growth by activating and practicing organization development.

ORGANIZATION DEVELOPMENT

What is organization development? Karen, a leader in a not-for-profit, recently told me her word picture for her role as an internal organization development consultant. She said,

> Imagine dry, rocky soil and a lone grapevine growing from the soil. Given enough water and some nutrients, the vine is able to grow and produce fruit, even though it is growing on the ground. However, being on the ground makes the plant vulnerable to insects and other

predators, and it is difficult for the vine and fruit to get adequate sunlight.

Now, imagine that I trained the vine to grow up a stake and along a wire supported by other stakes. The vine and fruit are off the ground. I still provide the appropriate nutrients and water. I also prune the vine to trim off branches that will not bear fruit and enable more sunlight to reach the other branches, leaves and fruit. This increases photosynthesis and brings energy to the whole plant, allowing normal ripening of the grapes. The plant flourishes. Taste the fruit; it is ripe and sweet.[1]

Karen's metaphor is apropos. Yes, an organization can survive and even produce fruit with only its natural growth (structure and systems evolving over time). But if it is going to flourish, organization architects like Karen need to eliminate waste (pruning) and implement innovations that release energy, resulting in an accomplished vision and the growth of each person in the organization.

Organization development is the continual practice of reflection, research, evaluation and change in order to efficiently and effectively accomplish the mission and vision and ensure that each member flourishes. Notice the first part of the definition. Change that truly addresses systemic problems and releases energy for flourishing must happen in the context of reflection, research and evaluation. This takes time, discipline and the multiple perspectives of people throughout the organization. A carefully crafted organization-wide effort to effectively achieve strategic goals is what organization development is all about.

TEN CHARACTERISTICS OF EFFECTIVE ORGANIZATION DEVELOPMENT

The following section identifies the characteristics of effective organization development.

1. The DNA lines up with the action plans. Donations plummeted at ABC Community Development Foundation during the 2008–2009 economic downturn. After adjusting the budget down 10 percent and laying off one staff member, the foundation still found their expenses unmanageable in light of decreased donations. The executive director decided to hire a fundraiser, George, who claimed he had a plan for raising money, especially since the foundation's focus was at-risk youth in the community. The fundraiser expressed this was an "easy sell" for people with money.

George planned a dinner at a five-star restaurant and invited his key contacts. Leading up to the event, he requested video and pictures of the youth. The program directors refused this request, since they had strong commitment to never portray the youth and their families in disrespectful ways or use the youth to obtain money. Knowing that George might not share their values, the directors also scripted what could and could not be said at the event so that the youth were not portrayed in a bad light. George ignored the directors and got photos from other staff not involved in the programs. At the dinner, he used his own script highlighting "the poor youth who needed money." The youth attending the event were humiliated and ashamed. They felt used. Their trust had been broken.

Fundraising like this that was not in line with the organization's values came close to derailing ABC's mission. Other quick fixes caused donations to continue to drop until a new executive director was hired.

Helen lived the DNA of ABC and acted swiftly to eliminate administrative waste and focus the employees on the heart of the mission, vision and values. Once the "house was in order," Helen unapologetically shared ABC's vision and outcomes with potential donors who identified with ABC's vision. Within six months, ABC's balance sheet was in the black.

Effective organization development occurs when the actions of an organization line up with its mission and values.

2. *Everyone contributes.* Effective development happens when all members of the organization know how they contribute to the mission and vision. It can't just be what is in the heads of the leadership. Everyone needs to embody the organization's values and have its sense of purpose. Training helps individuals know how to participate in the mission. Storytelling by veteran staff helps them gain a sense of what matters and the difficult or crazy things people were willing to do make it happen. Everyone is welcome to offer creative ideas for pressing forward toward their goals. The leadership makes sure people are given the opportunity to develop their skills and knowledge, which not only helps them personally but also helps the organization flourish.

3. Communication is open. When communication is open across departments and among peers, as well as vertically up and down the structure, the stage is set for organization development. If individuals or groups in organizations keep secrets and compete for resources, if they don't openly share facts and feelings, such unhealthiness will squelch growth. With the exception of confidential personnel issues, relatively little information should be kept secret. Transparency must be the goal in every aspect of the organization. Information is power. If only certain people in the organization have and hold information, organization development is not happening.

When Sherwood Lingenfelter became the dean of SWM (the School of World Mission, now the School of Intercultural Studies, at Fuller Theological Seminary), he learned that staff and faculty at Fuller felt the planning and budget process was mysterious and hard to understand. In fact, SWM faculty had the perception that the other schools, especially the School of Theology, received a larger portion of the revenue.

Lingenfelter learned that the perception that SWM received a smaller portion of the revenue was a myth and sought to bring to light the yearly budget process. He transparently shared the seminary's budget process and figures to debunk the myth. He also increased participation in the budgeting process by involving staff and faculty in planning and brainstorming cost-saving activities. Lingenfelter "solved" the mystery of the budget and planning process, and as a result, eliminated budget managers' propensity to hide money or accuse others of having a larger portion of overall revenue. Everyone knew the budget and how money was allocated. SWM staff and faculty felt empowered because of the transparency and invitation to participate.

4. Those with relevant and direct knowledge make decisions. Enterprise Rental Cars released a new commercial in which various staff repeat the phrase, "I will make it right!" Subsequently, if anything is wrong in a customer's experience of renting a car from Enterprise, a staff person has the authority and responsibility to fix the situation without asking a supervisor, without proposing a new project, without long waits for decisions from already-busy people.

Kicking problems upstairs to people who are actually removed from the situation reduces organization development. Those who are closest to a problem should be the primary instigators of strategy. They know the situation; they have the most relevant knowledge; therefore, their strategies, rather than those conceived at a distance, will likely be most effective.

J. Hudson Taylor established China Inland Mission (CIM, which became OMF International) after experiencing the untenable situation of leaders living in Great Britain directing ministry activities in China. Letters containing funding and permission for ventures minimally took three months by boat to arrive in China, and this was after the letter for requests took three months to reach Great Britain. Therefore, when Taylor began CIM, he adopted the value of leadership within context. Personnel in the various provinces of China had the most direct and relevant information and were therefore released to create strategies appropriate for their situation. This principle is still in effect in OMF International today.

5. Organizational health is rewarded and reinforced. Next, effective development occurs when an organization is healthy. What does organizational health look and feel like? Certainly it means people participate meaningfully in accomplishing the vision. It means the organization is creative, adaptable and innovative.

One key way to sustain this is by rewarding people appropriately. In most churches and Christian, nonprofit organizations, rewards are not likely to be financial. Individuals can't participate in stock options and bonuses are unlikely. But there are effective ways to help people who do well to feel appreciated. You can give public recognition or informally tell stories "around the water cooler" about jobs well done. Saying thank you and writing encouraging notes is also important. Giving gifts is another option. Leaders can also delegate more responsibility or provide more training or educational opportunities. Offering extra time off can be another bonus to consider.

When you reward people, keep two things in mind. First, remember that one size does not fit all. Some people thrive on public recognition while others are mortified by it. Some love gifts while others need a word of thanks or encouragement. Others think words are cheap and want recognition by being given more responsibility. Suit the reward to the person. Second, make sure the rewards are for what actually contributes to organizational health.

Every May, St. Stephens arranges a celebratory banquet to thank members of the congregation who participated in the children's and youth ministries throughout the year. Stories are told of the tireless work of a handful of volunteers who lead these ministries. The banquet ends with a call for others to commit to the programs for the following year. During the past three years, the pastoral team noticed that the number of persons signing up for these ministries decreased. This leaves them in the precarious position of begging congregants to volunteer when the school year begins in September. Exploring the issue further, Jane, the senior pastor, discovered people felt they could not contribute at the level of the "tireless" handful of volunteers and thus were reluctant to participate. The "reward," exemplified by the hard-working stories, actually discouraged organizational health rather than promoted it.

6. *Conflict is resolved constructively.* Hidden or ignored conflict can be deadly. But dealing with conflict in a way that leads to reconciliation gives life. Where organization development is working, conflict is used to stimulate innovation. The best ideas build on disagreements.

Recently Global Partners, a multinational organization, appointed a new international director for strategy. Joshua's task was to oversee worldwide strategy development. While he was an excellent innovator and had catalyzed several indigenous organizations, he could not transfer those experiences to his new director role. He became heavy handed with those he supervised, nitpicking the grammar and spelling of reports when not all of his team spoke English as a first language, feeling threatened by questions or suggestions, and demanding full allegiance without earning trust.

The staff tried to talk with Joshua, but these conversations increased his defensiveness and subsequent bad behavior. He wrote threatening emails to his team or did not communicate at all. The situation worsened until finally Joshua's team resigned en masse. Sensing his failure, Joshua also resigned after only being in the position for one year. But the damage had been done. Trust plummeted and new ministry initiatives stalled.

Unresolved conflict sucks up organizational energy in huge quantities. Many hours of internal dialogue and worry rob leaders of creativity and joy in their jobs. This propensity may actually be worse in churches and Christian organizations. Christians often mistakenly think that conflict is a sign of sin or a lack of love or patience. It's just not being "nice" somehow.

We may assume people will change if just given enough pastoral care and second chances. And that may be true. Many conflict problems can be resolved with training, love and creating a safe environment. But clear feedback and guidance toward truth is still necessary. Addressing conflict or bad behavior is uncomfortable. There's no getting around that. Being a leader means entering that awkward, uncomfortable zone for the purpose of growth and to accomplish the mission.

7. Processes and structures flow from the organization's DNA and its current needs. After the success of Saddleback Church and the books *The Purpose Driven Life* and *The Purpose Driven Church* by Rick Warren, I noticed churches around the world adopted Saddleback's leadership and training structures. Certainly the principles of these books are powerful if applied contextually. However, rote application of the structures was inappropriate for many situations due to their cultural context or the church's stage of growth. Pastors wanted fruit, so they adopted a methodology that worked elsewhere rather than prayerfully pursuing God's purpose for their church in context. The quick fix was not the right fix, as was the case for Vision Fellowship in Manila. Based on his observations of church life in Canada where he studied, Rico implemented small group meetings in homes in neighborhoods around the city along with a Sunday celebration service. Families were to meet in their home group for Bible study, fellowship and outreach. The small groups met several times, but little by little dwindled in attendance. Presuming the lack of attendance was due to weak leadership, Rico restructured the home groups, making sure that two strong leaders served each group. Numbers continued to shrink. Rico passionately preached the importance of small group accountability every Sunday morning, to no avail. The small groups did not grow. After six months of pushing, Rico learned from a brave young man that he couldn't attend home group because of his intense work and school commitments. After a fourteen-hour day, he didn't have the strength to attend small group, and this was the situation for most at Vision Fellowship. Yet for most members, their Sundays were free. Rico decided to experiment with the Sunday service, making it shorter in order to leave more time for small groups to meet for lunch and fellowship after the service. The small groups also focused their Bible study around application of the sermon, thus integrating what they had already heard in the service. The small groups thrived and multiplied.

8. *Success and innovation are rewarded; people learn from failure.* Brené Brown highlighted a significant fact in a recent TED talk.[2] She noted that all those who speak at TED conferences have failed in significant ways. They experimented with ideas, many times over and over again, and failed. But they learned from their mistakes, tried again and eventually experienced breakthrough.

Organization development thrives in contexts where people feel safe to offer ideas, take risks and fail. Breakthrough solutions emerge when people learn from failure and pursue creativity. Effective leaders create these environments of freedom and encourage innovation and experimentation.

Kim was a new production line manager overseeing a printing press. She was responsible for a $5,000 job that required delivering twenty thousand fliers by the end of the week, and she came through. The only problem was they were all wrong. The customer rejected the shipment because of an incorrect color. Kim was afraid she was going to be fired. But her boss, Juan, told her,

"Kim, why should I fire you? I just invested $5,000 in your training. Who else could I hire with that kind of experience? I know you will never make that mistake again." And Juan was right. Because of an environment where a single failure was not cause for termination, Kim became one of Juan's best managers.

9. People know their context. Organization development means connecting effectively with the outside world. Presumably, most churches exist for people who are not yet a part of a church. Ironically, many churches have no idea what the needs, concerns or makeup of their surrounding community is like. Yet because churches exist for others, it is imperative that members know what is going on around them and know the people in their communities that they are trying to serve.

Keiko, a church planter in Japan, reads cutting-edge technology, news, and university magazines, journals and blogs in order to stay aware of her context. She meets with other pastors once a month to discuss what they are learning about their ever-changing society. They discuss together what this means for outreach and discipleship strategies. Sometimes they invite twenty-somethings to talk about how they use social media and other trends. In their study and conversations, the Holy Spirit gives insight for how their witness attracts the Japanese.

10. Quick response to opportunities is made possible with lean procedures. In one of my classes several years ago I asked, "How long does it take you to get approval for a new project?" Sherman responded, "About one year. First, I need to write the project proposal within the guidelines my organization has established. Then I send the proposal to regional headquarters, and they give their input. Once I make changes based on their feedback, I send the proposal to the state headquarters, and they interact with the proposal and give their input. After adjustments—actually, sometimes the proposal doesn't even look like mine at this point—I send the proposal to divisional headquarters and hopefully get approval to proceed ahead with the project."

In most situations, waiting one year is too long. Healthy organizations find ways to make good decisions without undue delay in order to respond to their contexts. OMF International's approach to strategy development discussed in chapter five enables quick responses to contextual opportunities. As highlighted, decisions regarding strategy, activities and programs are made "in the field" by those with the most contextual knowledge rather than from a distance using layers of decision-making hierarchy.

> ### Stop and Think
>
> Write down some brief responses to the following:
> - Of the ten principles listed in this chapter, which ones does your organization practice well? Explain.
> - Which one or two of the ten principles are you weakest in? Why?
> - Write a SMARTER goal related to the one or two weak characteristics you identified.
> - What patterns or processes have worked best when considering a change in strategies or tactics? Try to notice the changes that produced life and flourishing.

How can we put all this into practice? How can assessing and implementing the discipline of organization development work for us? That's what chapter eight is all about.

8

MAKING ORGANIZATION DEVELOPMENT WORK FOR YOU

I asked the pastoral team of Hope Community Church to list all the activities (programs, services, outreach and ministries) the team, other staff and members of Hope engaged in. We filled flip-chart pages and displayed them on walls. I then asked the team to wander around the room and read all the activities to make sure we captured everything. After writing all the activities, I displayed the vision and mission of the church and asked the team to do three things: (1) to draw a line through any activity that did not connect with the vision and mission; (2) to place a star by the activities that are essential for doing the mission and accomplishing the vision; and (3) to place an "x" by the activities that are supportive of the essential activities.

This exercise allowed the team to assess overall progress toward the mission and vision in a number of ways. First, they saw that some programs were not essential to or supportive of the mission and vision. They discussed eliminating these ministries, especially given the church's finite resources. Of course this was easier said than done. They realized that most of these programs and activities had been initiated by core members pursuing their own visions or who had donated money to start a ministry. How would they cope with the disappointment and potential anger if they eliminated these programs?

Second, the team at Hope pinpointed nonnegotiable activities critical for accomplishing the vision. They not only decided to keep these activities, they proposed a plan to evaluate them regularly to consider ways to increase their effectiveness.

Third, they noticed a very high level of commitment to some supportive activities. Some leaders treated these activities as essential for the vision and mission. One example of this was a five-weekend membership and leadership course that was required for members who wanted to lead a particular ministry. Those at Hope who ran the five-weekend course opposed any other options for achieving the same ends—especially if it meant people didn't have to attend the course. In their minds, the course was an unchangeable, essential aspect of the mission. A support strategy had become confused with the mission.

The group also evaluated the support functions to see if they were efficient, ran smoothly and included evaluation processes. For example, the planning and budgeting process did not include evaluating whether or not each activity was still directly connected to the vision and mission. Rather, each year's budget was built primarily from the previous year's history.

Finally, the group saw that to make progress toward the vision, they would need to create some new support structures, such as a new website, a database and an e-learning platform.

Hope Community Church engaged in what is sometimes called a "function audit." That can sound a bit intimidating, but this sort of exercise is actually straightforward, easy to implement and normally inspiring and energizing for participants.

The exercise may reveal, however, significant programs, strategies or operations that need to be changed or entirely eliminated so the mission and vision can be achieved more effectively. When that happens, it usually means loss for someone. And loss can feel threatening even when everyone agrees the change should happen. Thus, organization development must always include a pastoral heart and posture. As Max De Pree says, "leaders must connect voice and touch."[1]

The method used with Hope Community Church to put organization development into practice was inductive. They started with everything the church was doing and worked back toward the vision. But there is another equally valid way to proceed. You can begin with the vision and on a clean slate without any essential reference to the past, work out the specifics of what fulfilling the vision would look like. That's what I did with Japan Link, a church-planting agency in Japan.

First, I wrote the key words or phrases of the vision statement for Japan Link at the top of flip-chart papers and hung them on walls around the room. Second, I divided the participants into as many groups as there were flip-chart pages (in this case, seven groups). Third, I asked each group to review the vision words and write the essential activities that would lead to fulfilling that word or phrase.

After three to five minutes, the groups rotated to the next paper and added more essential activities until participants had thoroughly worked out the implications of the words or phrases at the top of each paper without repeating activities. As a whole group, we then stood before each of the papers and chose the most essential activities. After these selections, we made a list of supportive functions needed to accomplish the essential activities. This whole process enabled the leaders of Japan Link to establish accountability systems and prioritize organization development toward accomplishing the vision.

The inductive approach can be especially helpful if you suspect your team is doing too many things that only marginally contribute toward the mission and which may need to be eliminated. The deductive method can be useful if you need to break out of old ways of thinking and develop some fresh ideas.

> ### Stop and Think
>
> Think about your team, department or organization. Which do you need more: fresh ideas to help you move forward, or to cut back on activities so you can focus on what is most important? Explain.
>
> Depending on your answer, consider taking an inductive or deductive approach to assessing your group's efforts.

Regular evaluation and assessment is essential if you are going to flourish. It can start with reviewing the ten characteristics of organization development as we did at the end of chapter seven. Taking stock of which activities best fulfill the mission is also important, as both Hope Community Church and Japan Link found.

CAPACITY DEVELOPMENT

Leading up to the International Council[2] of 2006, OMF International seemed primed for growth. All members shared the vision for "indigenous biblical church movements," and they had worked hard to intentionally develop godly, competent leaders in every context. As the time for the council approached, the leaders of OMF asked each of the sixteen countries represented to research and determine how many new members would be needed to bring ministry to the next level. Each field gave a target figure for personnel, and at the council an additional 20 percent were added for support personnel. Rounding the figures, the directors felt led to pray for nine hundred new workers and strategized to develop the capacity needed to effectively welcome, train and absorb these new members.

Another aspect of organization development is capacity development ("capacity building," as some refer to it). This involves the ongoing process of learning and developing attitudes, skills, resources and infrastructure to efficiently and effectively carry out the mission and vision. Here are the simultaneous activities OMF International engaged in to build capacity to move forward with their plans.

Driving the need to add substantially to their teams were new strategic initiatives. Realizing that people from East Asia (the focus of OMF's mission) had migrated far beyond the bounds of East Asia, OMF leaders formed new teams that ministered in cities with large concentrations of East Asian peoples. This even included a team that would work among the Chinese in Africa. Also, since many OMFers connect in their contexts through businesses, a missional business initiative with support systems was formed. OMF leaders knew that to do this they would need to identify and release entrepreneurs who had the ability to begin new efforts from scratch.

The member development director increased efforts to make sure OMF's DNA permeated recruitment, orientation and leadership training. After an initial review of the culture and language learning processes in each country, the member development (MD) team worked out best practices to effectively equip new missionaries in each setting.

While this was taking place, the director expanded the primary MD team and the number of trainers throughout the organization, especially those related to the essential functions of accomplishing the vision and mission. They conducted numerous training-the-trainer events so their work could be multiplied.

Finally, the MD team held organizational leaders workshops designed for the leadership teams of each country. In a yearlong process, these workshops provided organization development training through coaching, materials and action-learning projects. Each team attending the workshop chose a significant organizational challenge that needed breakthrough to advance the ministry. With all these resources, each team implemented a change strategy that tackled their challenges.

As this was going on, the personnel department studied attrition rates, discovering that 6 percent of OMFers left per year. Subsequently, they increased initiatives that supported workers in their various contexts, such as mobilizing teachers who served homeschooling families and encouraging centers to have member-care coordinators.

The mobilization and personnel departments gathered feedback from new workers regarding the application and candidature process. In most countries, paper applications were used in a lengthy, inefficient process. Applicants jokingly said OMF stood for "one million forms!" To remedy these problems, OMF developed a web-based system for every aspect related to personnel. This enabled people to receive appointments faster because mobilizing and ministry units were able to view applications simultaneously. The system also provided a platform for communication, sharing information and eventually, elearning.

Knowing that the initial orientation and ongoing training would be key to OMF's growth, the facilities of the international headquarters in Singapore were upgraded and expanded. Guest and training rooms, offices, the kitchen and the dining area were either added or remodeled to better host events.

All these activities, in addition to publishing prayer guides, enabled OMF to develop capacity in order to accommodate new workers. At the time of this writing, OMF has grown to the largest in its history—over fourteen hundred members.

OMF saw that it needed to target capacity building in multiple spheres at once—infrastructure (technology and facilities), leader development, mobilization, media, strategic initiatives and equipping—to accomplish its vision and mission of planting and developing "indigenous church and missions movements." Obviously a huge investment in resources was needed for the organization to grow. By use of some financial reserves and through prayer for the rest, all the initiatives were fully funded.

A PROCESS FOR CAPACITY DEVELOPMENT

That's how OMF International went about building capacity development. Let's break the steps down one by one.

Discerning the target. To build capacity, leaders require a full picture of the future, fulfilled vision. They must envision what will be seen, heard, felt and experienced if they have a flourishing organization. To achieve this, I suggest two exercises: faith-imagined future and organization-specific flourishing.

A faith-imagined future facilitates this process through four steps pictured in figure 8.1.

1. Thoroughly describe what will be seen, heard, felt and experienced when the vision

is accomplished. In a group setting, allowing for as much participation as possible, people describe what it will look like when the vision has happened, using phrases such as, "We will see..." and "People who encounter our organization will..." Remember, vision is results and outcomes oriented.
2. Identify the major themes of the accomplished vision. These are the key results that demonstrate the vision has been achieved.
3. Imagine what will be seen just before the vision is accomplished. What outcomes will have already happened just before the vision is achieved?
4. Continue working backwards in time, describing each stage of reaching the vision until the present time.

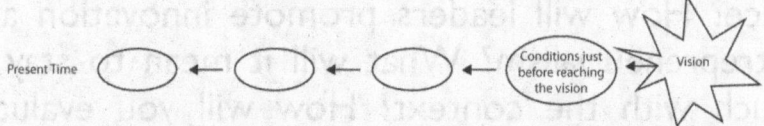

Figure 8.1. The process of faith-imagined future

This process, while somewhat complex, is powerful. Working from the present without describing future outcomes may cause teams to overlook important strategies or means that must be in place for the overall vision. For example, leader development is often overlooked or undervalued as people pursue vision. By engaging in this exercise, you can better determine how many leaders will be needed to fulfill the vision. Then you can strategize ways to replicate and develop the required number of leaders. A faith-imagined future enables people to do what is effective in the present in order to reach the future.

The second exercise for discerning the target is by describing your unique flourishing organization. In a similar manner to the other exercise, the faith-imagined future, picture your team or department as fully flourishing. Go back to chapter one and review the particulars of a flourishing organization. What will you see, feel, believe? What will you experience if your organization is vibrant and maturing? How will the DNA be inculcated and multiplied? How will new people be attracted and incorporated into the organization? What operations will be in place? How will leaders promote innovation and entrepreneurialism? What will it mean to stay in touch with the context? How will you evaluate strategies?

Assessment. The processes described in the previous exercises provide developmental insight for stages in accomplishing the vision. With your group's target fully pictured and steps toward that picture described, it is possible to then describe each developmental stage and identify critical areas for growth. Then evaluate all this in light of the ECO model from chapter two.

Of course, you can also use the inductive or deductive approach mentioned earlier in this chapter.

Planning and training. With the analysis accomplished, leaders are now ready to determine a way forward for capacity development which requires focus on multiple areas at once. What new, creative strategies will be needed to advance the mission? Are the members of the organization fully equipped to grow the organization and accomplish the vision? If not, what training is needed? What systems or structures will support growth? What technological innovations will enable sharing and accountability? Assuming specific initiatives, what resources (expertise, personnel and funding) will be required to pursue plans for capacity building?

Evaluation. With answers to the previous questions in hand, finish the capacity development process by writing measurable goals. "We know we have accomplished capacity development when..." This constant push toward defining and refining results enables leaders to stay on track when many things are happening all at once.

Organizational development often evolves in reaction to circumstances or crises without research, careful study and intentional planning. We're back to quick fixes. This is fine in the early stages of an organization's growth. As the organization matures, however, more comprehensive effort is needed.

Returning to our grapevine metaphor of chapter seven, it takes effort to drive in stakes and string wire and wisdom to know the appropriate amount of nutrients. Pruning is scary and often painful. Yet all these efforts result in the release of energy and increased fruit that is ripe and sweet.

9

THE ECOSYSTEM OF FLOURISHING—CULTURE

James sat facing sideways to the group, arms and legs crossed. He couldn't believe they were rehashing team dynamics again. Compared to his previous leadership experiences as a faculty member and then president of a large university, this was his most challenging and draining team situation to date. Now in his sixties and dean of the School of Theology, why couldn't he just pursue his vision and finish what he had been called to do? Why were they wasting time with these seemingly endless meetings?

Mei Ling and Sarah tentatively walked into the faculty meeting, immediately noticing James's body posture. They joined Sung already seated at the table. Sung offered to pray and get the meeting started.

"Well, I have been looking forward to talking about our new curriculum," Sung began. "Hopefully we can clear up some misunderstandings. Mei Ling, James didn't mean to exclude you by working on the design of the new curriculum for the Theology MA. It's just that he has had a lot of experience. He just wants to get on with the development."

"James, do you really feel that we are preventing you from carrying out your vision, as you stated in your email?" Sarah asked. "Do you think we are somehow 'blocking' you?"

"James, I'd be curious to know what your vision is," Mei Ling offered. "You never really shared that with us. Is it different from the vision we have had in this school for seven years? Your email regarding vision was the first that we have heard you talk about vision. And I'm not sure I really know what that vision is."

"I have been given a mandate from the board," James said, "to incorporate leadership materials into our curriculum. That is my vision."

"Well, maybe you could help us understand what you mean by incorporating leadership materials," said Sung. "Are you saying that the current materials do not incorporate leadership modules?"

"It's like what I did for class last quarter," James responded.

"But the course notes weren't changed for last quarter," Mei Ling said. "There were just a few edits."

"Yes," James agreed, "but I gave five one-hour lectures focused on leadership."

"And those were great lectures," Mei Ling noted quickly.

"But we also need to think through how to make input like that interactional," added Sarah. "Our professors have learned that adults do not necessarily remember what they have heard. They need to do something in order to learn."

"There you go again with your adult-learning theory." James's frustration was showing through. "This is why I can't carry out my vision. I feel chained by the need to be interactive. I lecture. That is what I do."

"Yes, and we love your lecturing!" Sarah affirmed. "It's just that we do not know how to incorporate this style of lectures into the curriculum or make them reproducible for others to teach the material. We want students to learn the material and immediately reproduce it in their own contexts."

"We've gone through this again and again," James said. "You don't respect my training and experience. I am called to do something in this school."

Mei Ling began showing her feelings too. "Yes! And we're called to do something as well! And we've been on this faculty long before you arrived. Our experience is valid also."

James was fed up. "This takes too much time and energy. I can't stand these meetings. I am drained. We are never going to finish the curriculum."

Everyone fell silent and eventually went back to their offices. Later in the day, Sarah, Sung and Mei Ling discussed what to do now that they knew how James really felt. After five months of working with him, they couldn't understand his lack of communication and reticence to collaborate. Now they understood that James felt more comfortable telling them what to do while he pursued "his vision." Actually, as a team they believed in James's vision and wanted to help him bring it to fruition. At the same time, they knew James was only in this leadership position for two years, so they wanted to help him implement the vision so it would be reproducible after he was gone. And they were used to collaboration and working as a team, especially when developing new curriculum.

After James's blow up, Sarah, Sung and Mei Ling were afraid for their jobs. Would James insist that they go? What would James report to the board? And what should they do about the already scheduled classes—some starting in the next week? Did James have other materials he wanted them to use?

On the following Monday, Sarah, Sung and Mei Ling decided they needed to talk with someone. Because of James's esteemed position in the school, they had not shared with anyone the strong emails and conversations they had had with James. Now they went to one of the vice presidents and told their story, especially their most recent encounter with James. After hearing the way they were treated, the vice president encouraged them to talk with the provost, since he was James's supervisor. The team was reluctant to do this, so the vice president agreed to talk with the provost first on their behalf.

A few days later, the provost stopped by Sarah, Sung and Mei Ling's office to listen to their story. He assured them their jobs were not in jeopardy, and he told them he would talk with James. They felt relieved that someone in leadership knew what was going on and waited, but as the weeks went by, there was no further interaction with the provost, and their relationships with James continued to disintegrate.

ORGANIZATIONAL CULTURE

Organizational culture powerfully determines the success or failure of a vision, the flourishing or demise of the human spirit. The story of James highlights the clash of at least three, if not more, cultural values and assumptions. As the dean, James expects a responsive team, ready to implement *his* vision. He is not used to being questioned by those he supervises and to taking so much time for team meetings and relationship building. He has a task, and he wants to "get on with it."

But the team's organizational culture is highly participative and assumes that James, like the previous dean, will work in collaboration as well as maintain their teaching philosophy of reproducibility and adult-learning focus. The team thrives in the creative process of curriculum development and continually asks, How can we do this better?

The provost of the school has established an organizational culture that presumes respect for elders and those in authority as well as harmony. Therefore, he talks briefly with James and does not confront the situation, assuming it will naturally resolve itself.

The clash of these organizational cultures and their manifest expectations leaves confusion and a stalled vision. As a result, Sarah, Sung and Mei Ling's years of effective work potentially derails, and James is intensely discouraged.

DEFINITIONS

Organizational culture can loosely be defined as the shared assumptions, beliefs and normal behaviors (norms) of a group. It has powerful influence on the way people live and act in an organization, department or team. Organizational culture dictates how and if people really belong. It determines what behaviors are deemed appropriate or not in the group context. Organizational culture shapes the strategies and subsequent activities the organization chooses to do in order to pursue its vision. Edgar Schein defines organizational culture as

> a pattern of basic assumptions—invented, discovered, or developed by a given group as it learns to cope with its problems of external adaptation and internal integration—that has worked well enough to be considered valid

and, therefore, to be taught to new members as the correct way to perceive, think, and feel in relation to those problems.[1]

Schein also says, "Organizational cultures are created by leaders, and one of the most decisive functions of leadership may well be the creation, the management, and—if and when that may become necessary—the destruction of culture."[2]

As I indicated in previous chapters, the ECO model clarifies connections between the seen—policies, procedures, structure, etc.—and the unseen—faith assumptions and values—elements in organizations. Likewise, organizational culture is an interaction of both seen and unseen elements. Schein labels the visible elements "artifacts," which can be buildings, office layouts, art, documents, the way people dress, as well as what one observes in people's interactions and relationships. For Schein, there are also the deeper levels of the unseen—values (creeds, slogans, code of ethics, etc.) and assumptions (default modes, sacred cows, unspoken rules, etc.).[3] Remember, values and assumptions influence and are embodied in behavior; likewise, behavior influences and forms values and assumptions—a constant feedback loop.

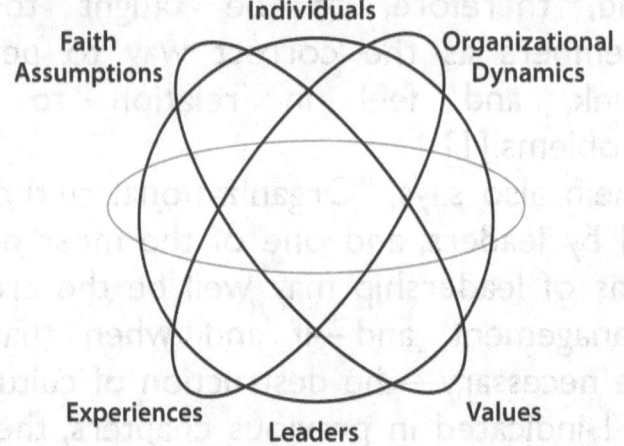

Figure 9.1. Organizational culture

For this book, the critical question we must ask as we engage organizational culture is, What environment promotes flourishing? What culture enables people to thrive? What culture enables the overall team to thrive in such a way that they accomplish the vision? Or, alternatively, what organizational culture destroys human flourishing or squelches vision?

Stop and Think

Jot down some responses to the following:
- Remember a time when you flourished. What factors in the environment, the organizational culture, promoted your flourishing?
- Notice those around you. When do they flourish? What factors in the organizational culture contribute to their flourishing?

> • In your experience, what aspects of organizational culture destroy human flourishing or squelch vision?

James Collins's research indicates that truly great organizations have cultures that dance between a "culture of discipline" and an "ethic of entrepreneurship."[4] People operate in freedom, innovating, inculcating their DNA and fanatically pursuing the vision. There is no need for tyrannical, dictatorial leadership or rules, since the discipline and entrepreneurialism live in the culture, in each person. This sounds like the culture Jesus created among his disciples—to which we now turn.

JESUS CULTURE

Schein's research indicates that leaders are the primary creators and shapers of organizational culture. What leaders teach, model, pay attention to, how they deal with crises, measure, reward and sanction—all these establish organizational culture.[5]

In three short years of ministry, Jesus established a new culture of flourishing—in individual lives and in a movement that would change the world. As noted in chapter one, Jesus followed a mandate and pattern anticipated by the prophet Isaiah:

The Spirit of the Lord is upon me,

> because he has anointed me
> to bring good news to the poor.
> He has sent me to proclaim release to the captives
> and recovery of sight to the blind,
> to let the oppressed go free,
> to proclaim the year of the Lord's favor.
> (Lk 4:18-19; cf. Is 61:1-2; 58:6)

Jesus infused life in such powerful ways that previously ostracized, ordinary, now-transformed men and women became the leaders of a worldwide movement. What was this new culture of flourishing and how did Jesus, as the leader, establish it? What did Jesus teach, model, pay attention to, measure and reward in order to create a flourishing movement? A comparison of the culture Jesus created and his cultural milieu offers insights for our own efforts to create environments of flourishing. While I extrapolate somewhat in table 9.1 based on New Testament history, I believe there is enough evidence to ascertain a sense of the culture formed by Jesus in contrast to his context. Remember, leaders form culture through teaching and modeling, as well as by what they pay attention to, measure and reward.

Given these insights, imagine the following:
- What would you experience if Jesus was the leader of your organization?

- What might you feel?
- How would you belong?
- How would you know whether or not you belong?
- What would happen if you failed or did something wrong?
- What might happen if you succeeded?

Jesus founded a community that was so life focused and full of life, it naturally grew to incorporate others and became an attractive, infusive, worldwide movement. Jesus manifested and demonstrated God's compassionate response to the calamities and suffering in human existence.

Table 9.1. Jesus culture

Culture Formation	Cultural Context	Jesus
Relationship with God	• God's presence is mediated through temple and priests as set out in Torah. • The coming eschaton and Messiah will come when the faithful follow the law and cease from their sin. • The Roman and Greek cultures appease various gods through rituals and by offering sacrifices.	• Jesus is the new temple where heaven and earth meet, where we can find new intimacy with God. • Jesus himself fulfills the law for his people. His followers obey in loving response to what God in Christ has already done. • Considers his followers to be friends, no longer servants. He encourages them to not be afraid but to have faith in God.
Relationship with Others	• Status determined by relationship. Necessary to keep within the rules of one's social designation. • Strict social rules of association; exclude "sinners." • Complex system of obligation and reciprocity.	• Highly relational. Travels, eats, sleeps, etc., with a wide variety of people—even cultural outcasts and women. • Interdependence—mutuality in giving and receiving. • Invites a wide variety of people to participate in his mission and gives them authority and power to do so.
Calling/Mission	• Appease gods in order to gain favor and protection. • Interpret the law and judge by observing blessing and cursing. • For Jews, usher in the Messianic reign and overthrow the Roman occupation by ensuring the community keeps the law. • For Romans, continue to amass wealth, military power and political power.	• Proclaims the kingdom of God and demonstrates God's reign. • Demonstrates the true heart and character of God who desires shalom—good news for the poor, healing, release from bondage, recovery of sight and salvation—and relationship. • Overcomes the power of sin and death through his death and resurrection. • Invites all to participate in God's kingdom and empowers them to do so.
Approach to Leadership	• Certain people lead, largely depending on birth and social status. • Leadership pattern tends to be authoritarian.	• Fishermen and other common people invited into leadership. • Encourages his followers to not be authoritarian (not to "lord it over" others as Gentile rulers do).
Posture toward Cultural Context	• Zealots sought to throw out the Romans by violence. • The Essenes responded to Roman occupation by withdrawing from society into remote communities. • Pharisees accommodated themselves to some aspects of Roman rule so they could have some independence of worship.	• Jesus reinterpreted the ultimate struggle as not being with Rome but with Satan. Ultimate power did not lie in political rule but in the kingdom of God. Power comes from God for the purpose of flourishing. This gives perspective as we confront evil in the world.
Measure/Pay Attention to/ Reward	• Externals: law keeping, the "right" way of behaving as interpreted by leaders. • Judging who is "in" and who is "out" by virtue of observed physical and spiritual health. • Those who are blessed have money, status and health.	• Responds to God's reign with obedience. • Faith, faithfulness and doing the acts of God in the kingdom of God. • Extends compassion and healing to those in physical and spiritual bondage. • Life-giving, life-flourishing.

As he approached the gate of the town, a man who had died was being carried out. He was his mother's only son, and she was a widow; and with her was a large crowd from the town. When the Lord saw her, he had compassion for her and said to her, "Do not weep." Then he came forward and touched the bier, and the bearers stood still. And he said, "Young man, I say to you, rise!" The dead man sat up and began to speak, and Jesus gave him to his mother. (Lk 7:12-15)

For those whose lives were languishing or squelched, whether because of demons, other spiritual, emotional or physical sicknesses or some combination of these, he offered release and participation in a fully flourishing life. This kingdom-of-God-oriented community was to partake fully in God's triune life and extend this life to others. Members of this community thrived and developed into their full humanity, as exemplified by Jesus. They were freed and empowered to extend God's compassion, healing and kingdom life to others. As we read in Luke, "Then Jesus called the twelve together and gave them power and authority over all demons and to cure diseases, and he sent them out to proclaim the kingdom of God and to heal" (Lk 9:1-2). Rather than subjected to rules creating boundaries and barriers, all were invited without reference to lineage or status and empowered to participate and extend kingdom life to others. We have yet to witness the full impact of flourishing, which will come in the new heaven and new earth.

Stop and Think

We can feel the powerful difference between these two cultures. Perhaps now is a good time to pause and evaluate our own leadership and the characteristics of organizational culture it establishes.

- How do we proclaim, live in and extend the reality of the kingdom of God?
- How, in our leadership, do we protect the brokenhearted, remove bondage, offer healing in its various forms, call others to participate in the kingdom and empower them to do so?
- Is our organization flourishing—growing, reproducing, becoming what it is meant to be—and fulfilling God's purpose for it?
- How much is there a climate of secrecy, fear, judgment and exactness? How is that evidenced?

Perhaps we can answer these questions by observing the lives of those we serve.

- Do we notice others transforming into the likeness of Christ? How?
- Are they free to risk, experiment, innovate and grow? How do they respond to failures?
- What are others learning?
- How do their lives impact others? Are others attracted to the flourishing lives they see?

I believe that Jesus' example of creating a culture of flourishing empowers us today. Therefore, in the following section I highlight his pattern, his method of establishing organizational culture.

JESUS ESTABLISHES AN ENVIRONMENT FOR FLOURISHING

As I read the Gospels, I see a pattern that includes four activities Jesus used to establish a kingdom-of-God-centered community.

1. Authentic engagement. Whether through natural (spending time, asking questions, eating, drinking and living together) or supernatural (words of knowledge and prophetic revelation) ways, Jesus knew how to connect with people's hearts. "He knew what they were thinking" (Lk 11:17). He understood what motivated people and what bound them. He knew what aspects of their lives needed healing and freedom. He under stood how to offer unique blessing to each individual. This authentic engagement enabled Jesus to touch people's lives and bring restoration.

In addition to authentically knowing individuals, Jesus desired them to know him and to let himself be known by others. He told the disciples, "I do not call you servants any longer, because the servant does not know what the master is doing; but I have called you friends, because I have made known to you everything that I have heard from my Father" (Jn 15:15). He straightforwardly revealed his purpose and plans and invited his friends to participate in the kingdom-of-God future. No secrecy. No hiddenness.

2. Invitation to participate. Even when full transformation has not occurred, Jesus invites people to live under his life-giving reign and join in extending this reign to others. When he saw the tax collector Levi in his tax booth, he called him to follow—even before Levi changed his life. It was Jesus' love, acceptance and calling that created the change (Lk 5:27-30). One only needs to follow Jesus and obey his lead. No special lineage, schooling, gender or social status is needed. Everyone can "play."

3. Empowerment. An invitation to participate is mute without the authority and empowerment to do so, and Jesus offers this as well. When sending the disciples to proclaim the kingdom of God, cast out demons and heal the sick, he gave them the ability to do so (Lk 9–10). And this was not to be temporary empowerment. Jesus and the Father send the Holy Spirit to live in disciples (Jn 14:15-16; Acts 1:8). In fact, the full triune life of God is available to dwell in believers (Jn 14:23). This indwelling means that we will be transformed, because when we see Jesus face to face, we will be like him. In this way we have the ability to live in and extend the kingdom to others.

4. *Corrects life-squelching beliefs, attitudes and actions.* The Pharisees were looking for something to accuse Jesus of. On the Sabbath, in the synagogue, they saw their chance. Would Jesus heal a man with withered hand? "Jesus said to them, 'I ask you, is it lawful to do good or to do harm on the sabbath, to save life or to destroy it?' After looking around at all of them, he said to [the man], 'Stretch out your hand.' He did so, and his hand was restored" (Lk 6:9-10).

Inevitably Jesus' actions, as interpreted by the Pharisees, were judged unlawful. Jesus used this conflict, however, to show God's intentions and correct anything that hindered full life. An exasperated Jesus calls the Pharisees hypocrites because they did not demonstrate God's heart with their lack of compassion and hope for healing for those who suffer (exemplified in the passage just quoted and in Lk 13:15). He demonstrated that many had lost sight of the reason behind so many rules. His people were to be subject only to the higher law of love for God and others.

Jesus formed a community that would change the world. His life and ways established a flourishing, reproducing movement. May God give us the grace and empowerment to form similar communities.

10

MAKING CULTURE WORK FOR YOU

Often we go about our work, day in day out, year in year out, without intentionally considering the environment we create. We could just start doing things we think will help. But if we want to avoid a quick-fix mentality to corporate culture, the place to start is envisioning an environment that enables people to flourish. What would it be like?

Here are three exercises you could use to get you started:

1. Think of a time when you would say that you grew like a weed. What were the circumstances that allowed you to learn rapidly? Tell the story to someone or write it down. Now go back and reflect on the story. What were the factors that enabled you to grow? Having a group of people do this exercise together invites flourishing, because they can see together what promotes growth in a range of people and experiences.

2. In a group setting, have individuals draw pictures of what comes to mind when they think of flourishing. Anything goes. It could be a nature scene, but it doesn't have to be. Next, have each person share and describe his or her picture. Based on the individual pictures, have the whole group draw or describe a picture that expresses flourishing. Finally, put the picture into words and write it down.
3. While exercise two focused on what flourishing looks like, this one focuses on what it feels like. Ask those involved to write down their responses. Then in the large group, ask people to share their answers and put them up on a board so everyone can see. After that, ask, "What, in your experience, has led to flourishing?" Note down these instances or stories. The process of picturing or identifying flourishing enables those in your organization to adopt behaviors that create flourishing environments.

After any one of the three exercises, a group can begin to develop concrete, specific activities, strategies and plans for building a new culture. Once you see what you are aiming at, it is easier to judge if any given idea will bring you closer to your goal.

TIME AUDIT

Since the formation of culture is so intimately connected with what leaders model—what they actually do—I encourage those I coach to monitor the way they spend their time in a normal week. In your diary, journal or on an Excel spreadsheet (it doesn't matter what you use as long as it is always accessible and can later be used for analysis), write down what you do every half hour. Yes, every half hour! At the end of the week, create specific categories for ways you spend time—exercise, emails, TV, meetings (include type), preparation, phone calls, prayer, Bible study, entertainment, commuting (what do you do when you commute?), hygiene, sleep, cooking, household chores and so forth. Tally the amount of time spent in each category. You should have a total of 168 hours for seven days. Leaving out the hours you sleep, assign percentages of time to each category. You may draw a pie chart or graph if you are helped by visuals.

Notice your sleep patterns first. What might they reveal about your heart and modeling? Like David, can you say, "I lie down and sleep; I wake again, for the Lord sustains me. I am not afraid of ten thousands of people who have set themselves against me all around" (Ps 3:5-6)? Are you getting adequate rest? Experts agree that most adults need eight to nine hours of sleep each night. Eight to nine hours allows enough time for the needed REM cycles, which are necessary for the brain to process and rest.

Now focus on the percentages of the other categories. What do you observe? Does any aspect of the way you spend time surprise you? What are you modeling? What values are revealed by how you spend your time? Ultimately we want to ensure that what we do matches what we say. Remember the cause-effect loops!

A number of years ago I coached Charlie, a pastor of a large church in the southern United States, and she conducted the time audit exercise. When we analyzed Charlie's typical week, we noticed that 75 percent of her time was spent in the office answering emails, updating projects' planning and progress, and preparing media for Sunday services. Yet Charlie espoused values of relationship and community. Something needed to change so that her espoused values matched her lived values.

Charlie increased the hours she met with the staff team and invited new, emerging leaders into project administration and preparation of media. Rather than doing her work alone, Charlie asked others to work with her. These changes were easily made with small adjustments.

Charlie went further, however, and reflected more deeply. She asked herself why she was choosing to spend 75 percent of her time alone in her office. We discovered deep fatigue and apathy; she was on the verge of burnout. Charlie shared with me that she had not had a vacation in several years and perhaps was addicted to activity. These realizations initiated a process that eventually led her to take a three-month sabbatical.

With the full blessing of the staff and congregation, Charlie created an autoreply for her email account that said she was not available for three months and offered the contact information of other leaders in the church. During the first month, Charlie mostly addressed her fatigue by sleeping as much as she wanted, exercising and eating healthy foods. After adequate rest, she felt ready to address her propensities toward the need to control and escape into work by seeing a spiritual director and therapist. At the same time, she continued her healthier physical habits and added manual projects around the house and yard. After the three months, Charlie felt more self-aware and able to establish patterns of work that were sustainable for the long haul. Her restoration enabled her to once again fully embrace her call, and now what she says she values matches her lived values. She is able to form a welcoming, highly relational community.

Stop and Think

Write down answers to the following:
- What do you value in your work and the rest of your life?

> Now conduct a seven-day time audit. Break down your hours by categories and percentages.
> • How do the results match or not match what you say you value?
> • What steps could you take to bring your values and how you spend your time more into alignment?

RESPONDING TO CRISIS OR CONFLICT

The formation of organizational culture is accelerated in crises and conflicts. When crisis hit Focus on Unreached Peoples (FUP), which we met in chapter one, the culture changed dramatically—and not for the good.

Another group exercise can be to think back to a significant crisis or conflict in your organization or leadership. If you know a particular recent crisis would be helpful to discuss, you might want to ask someone ahead of time to prepare a summary of the event. What led up to it? What were the circumstances surrounding the crisis? What did leadership do in the crisis? How were things handled or resolved? Were they resolved? Then ask others to add details they recall or offer other interpretations of what happened.

After you have relived the story, consider what organizational culture may have been formed because of leaders' responses in crisis. Did the responses bring freedom, transparency and hope? Control, secrecy or fear? Are there any aspects of this crisis that still need resolution? Are there negative cultural tendencies that may need to be addressed or changed? What behaviors or modeling would bring the changes?

PHYSICAL SPACE AND ARTIFACTS

Physical spaces reveal organizational culture. Knowing this offers the opportunity for discovery and intentional change. Here's another exercise, then. Take thirty minutes to sit in the space you consider best represents your organization (office, sanctuary, courtyard, etc.). Notice what you feel as you sit in the space. What is represented by how the office is laid out? By the art? By other visible artifacts? Reflect on how new people encounter the space. What do they feel? Is it easy to figure out where to go? Are they easily welcomed?

This is also something any team can discuss. What organizational culture do you want the physical space to communicate? As an administrator at Fuller, I once had the opportunity to design our office. When I started work in advising, the offices were partitioned with tall, portable, tan-colored walls that nearly reached the ceiling. Thus the internal offices were dismal and dark. The reception desk was off on one side, making it difficult for newcomers to immediately notice the reception and check in. The director stated that the high walls were in place for privacy reasons, which made sense since we were dealing with personal matters (individuals' stories, finances and grades).

When I became the director, we discussed as a team our vision and values. In general, we wanted students to feel welcome and encouraged. We wanted to come alongside in such a way that we could listen to students' journeys and then help them design an individual master's or doctoral program appropriate for their calling and future. We wanted to have an environment where students felt free to drop in and have a cup of coffee or tea.

Since our office was scheduled for an upgrade, we decided to incorporate our vision and values into the redesign. We made the reception the center the hub of the office. When people came in, we wanted them to be welcomed immediately. We took down the eight-foot, tan walls and replaced them with five-foot, purple-hued walls. The shorter walls allowed the sunlight from two walls of windows to come in, giving the space a light, airy feel. The beige carpet was replaced with multicolored purple carpet, and we selected art and fabrics from around the world for the walls. Overall, the office was beautiful and hospitable for our multinational student body. Even though the walls were only five feet tall, each cubicle space was large enough that, for the most part, conversations could not be overheard. We also played light music in the office, which covered voices. However, if students felt uncomfortable sharing, we adjourned to a conference room that was private.

Organizational culture is one of the most critical factors that determine whether or not individuals flourish. As such, it has direct impact on the mission and pursuit of the vision. The true values and assumptions of an organization are manifested in organizational culture. Organizational culture has the power to constrain strategy, identify who belongs and who does not, and most importantly, promote or hinder flourishing.

11

THE ECOSYSTEM OF FLOURISHING—STRUCTURE

The Bible does not mandate any one type of structure for organizations. Several different configurations are mentioned. Right after the people of Israel left Egypt, Moses was a one-man show. All decisions came to him. But Moses listened to the advice of his father-in-law and started delegating more. "Moses chose able men from all Israel and appointed them as heads over the people, as officers over thousands, hundreds, fifties, and tens" (Ex 18:25). This relieved Moses of an extreme administrative load. Even though the Israelites were now free from Egypt, they still needed structure so they could flourish. Structure would make it possible for the people to worship the Lord and become a blessing to all nations.

After Moses, the nation was led by a series of judges, the last of whom was Samuel. But the people wanted a different structure. They wanted to be led by a king like other countries. God didn't think this was a very good idea, but he granted the people their request. And after King Saul, David was not only king but a man after God's own heart. David was not just to be the ancestor of the Messiah but a model of the kind of leader the Messiah would become.

The early church had other structures. Paul and Barnabas appointed elders to lead the churches they established without any apparent mention of appointing a pastor to lead each church (Acts 14:23). We also see a structure of the church in Jerusalem providing leadership for the other churches in the region (Acts 15). Likewise Titus was appointed as a regional leader who had the responsibility to appoint elders in the towns of Crete who would oversee individual congregations (Tit 1:5).

Why were there different types of structures? Because the needs, circumstances and mission of each situation were different. In architecture, the saying goes, "Form follows function." When talking about organizations, "Structure follows mission and context."

In this chapter, after introducing the definition and purpose of organizational structure, I describe tendencies organizations have in how they structure themselves. Finally, I suggest key principles that guide structure formation and structural change processes.

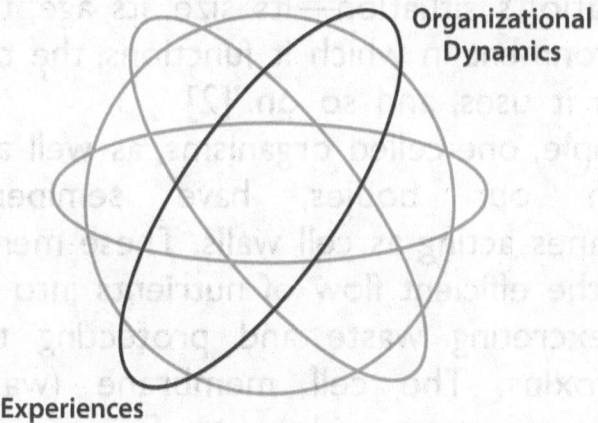

Figure 11.1. The organization action loop

WHAT ORGANIZATIONAL STRUCTURES ARE ALL ABOUT

Henry Mintzberg, Harvard professor and guru of organizational structures, defines organizational structure as "the sum total of the ways in which its labor is divided into distinct tasks and then its coordination is achieved among these tasks."[1] To his definition I always add, "so as to accomplish the organization's vision and enable flourishing." After all, that is the whole point of having structure.

Mintzberg goes on to say that structures should be dynamic, and that each organization should proactively strategize for structural changes in order to meet the needs of its environment. "The elements of structure should be selected to achieve an internal consistency or harmony, as well as a basic consistency with the organization's situation—its size, its age, the kind of environment in which it functions, the technical systems it uses, and so on."[2]

Simple, one-celled organisms, as well as every cell in our bodies, have semipermeable membranes acting as cell walls. These membranes enable the efficient flow of nutrients into the cell while excreting waste and protecting the cell from toxins. The cell membrane (wall) also provides structure and space for the nucleus, ribosomes, lysosomes and mitochondria. Likewise, organizational structures facilitate the flow of resources—funding and people—that in turn enable the mission to be accomplished. The questions we must all ask concerning organizational structure are, Is our structure helping or hindering movement toward fulfilling our vision? Also, does our structure embody our values?

We can evaluate the answer to these questions, for example, by observing how long it takes to get approval for a new project or venture due to an unexpected opportunity.

The tragedy of the Southeast Asian earthquake and tsunami of 2004 provided unexpected opportunities for connection and service in affected regions. As expatriates and locals suffered together, deeper relationships formed.

Stop and Think

> Take a moment to draw a picture of your organization's structure. Then reflect:
> - Is your organizational structure helping or hindering movement toward fulfilling the vision? How so?
> - In what ways does your organization's structure embody the values of the organization?
> - In what ways does your organization's structure promote or hinder flourishing?

Missionaries from the First Church denomination on the island of Phuket in Thailand decided to partner with locals to reconstruct homes and businesses. They also formed a school for English language acquisition. The purpose was to provide the Thai with the skills necessary to interact with and gain employment in the Western NGOs that came to Phuket after the tsunami.

The missionaries applied to the regional representatives of their denomination for permission and funding. The regional representatives, after editing and changing the proposal, forwarded it on to the denomination's board located in a Western country for approval. The board only met twice a year, and therefore the missionaries were in limbo until the board finally gave approval. However, by this point, the Thai friends of the missionaries had had to move off the island because they did not have the resources to rebuild and participate in new business ventures. The structure didn't help fulfill the denomination's mission. The structure prevented it.

Another company I encountered wanted to empower leadership throughout its membership. They thought each individual should determine the appropriate ways to accomplish their work. Yet interviews with members uncovered frustration. Top-level leaders had to give their approval for most initiatives, even seemingly small decisions such as the color of a training center. The level of frustration and cynicism can be a helpful measure in knowing how well core values are or aren't embodied in a structure.

If sharing resources is a core value for an organization, yet there is no mechanism to facilitate the sharing, then the structure is not enabling the fulfillment of the value. If leading from a particular context is a stated value, yet approval from central leadership is required for strategy and finances, the structure is a hindrance to the value.

In general, Christian organizations have a tendency to undervalue or dismiss the need to evaluate their structure unless there is a crisis, and then the tendency is to implement a quick fix. Along with Mintzberg, I encourage a more deliberate, proactive approach to structures. Before getting into that, let me outline a number of approaches I have observed in Christian organizations concerning structure.

ORGANIZATIONAL STRUCTURES AND TENDENCIES IN CHRISTIAN ORGANIZATIONS

Here are six approaches I observe in Christian organizations toward organizational structures—four undesirable and two desirable.

1. Structure by tradition. Sometimes Christians assume that their structure was God-initiated—at least at one point in time—and should therefore always remain intact. Denominational polity is one such example. Even if members of the organization do not view the structure as God-initiated, because it has always worked in the past or is comfortable, it remains unevaluated and unchanged for years and years. Tradition is the high value.

Given what I have already stated about structures, one can surmise a number of problems with this approach to organizational structures. First, structuring by tradition often prevents the organization from knowing, connecting to and engaging with its environment. The world around them changes, but the organization does not respond. As a result, it becomes inward focused and unable to meet the needs for which it exists.

Second, the organization loses its ability to adapt to an ever-changing context. This inflexibility saps innovation, making it difficult to accomplish the vision. Third, often a long-term structure becomes too cumbersome. This happens when organizational leaders make small adjustments to the structure, quick fixes, which quite often add layers and burdensome requirements for projects and programs. With these tweaks that do not address the whole system, planning, budgeting and approval processes become long and arduous.

The three-school structure at Fuller Theological Seminary naturally evolved as each school was founded at different points in time. As the School of Psychology and the School of World Mission were added to the School of Theology, each school implemented its own academic, administrative, budget and revenue structures. The three schools did, however, share for the most part admissions, registration and finance procedures.

Since each faculty governed each school, the schools were free to grow and expand within the boundaries of the seminary mission, "to prepare men and women for the manifold ministries of Christ and the Church." New degree programs, regional campuses and distance-learning programs were added, and the seminary grew to be the largest evangelical seminary in the world while the structure essentially remained the same. Each school governed themselves independently, some would say in isolation, of the other schools. One sad, oft-used phrase exemplified this separation: "The only thing connecting the three schools of Fuller Seminary are the pipes." That was, until the economic downturn in 2008.

Because of the recession, the Fuller Foundation's endowment investments plummeted, which decreased the drawdown funds available for operations. This led to a significant and extreme structural analysis that revealed departmental redundancies and waste. The schools had simply grown in isolation without overall assessment. The consequences of the analysis were painful. To eliminate redundancies and encourage better efficiency, 10 percent of senior administrators and staff were laid off, and departments were combined to form new entities. The losses were extremely threatening, especially for those who had always "done it this way." Facing the challenges together, however, a new vision of "One Fuller" was promoted, effectively breaking down the walls between the three schools. New cooperation and collaboration revitalized the institution.

2. Structure by the chart. Wolfgang became the leader of a church-planting ministry in Vietnam. During my first visit for coaching, I noticed an extensive organogram taped to his wall. I asked Wolfgang about the diagram. He smiled at me and said, "That is the future!" Observing closer, I saw that in addition to church-planting teams, Wolfgang had included positions such as business manager, third-culture-kids coordinator, placement and orientation coordinator, area directors, administrators and so on. While I applauded Wolfgang's vision, I encouraged him to hold the chart loosely, since year-by-year contextual factors, opportunities and growth may dictate a different approach to their structure.

With the structure-by-chart approach, organizational leaders draw an organogram and then seek to fill the positions on the chart. The diagram portrayed on the chart determines the structure, without reference to the vision or the context. Also, when someone leaves a job and the position is empty, supervisors hire to fill the vacancy without evaluation as to whether or not the position is still needed.

The negatives of this approach are similar to structure by tradition. There are too many variables, and constant evaluation is necessary. When a position is vacant, leaders must ask, Is this position still needed for the current realities of the context? For efficiency, should the position be eliminated? Or perhaps the responsibilities and functions of the position have grown and actually two or three positions are needed rather than one.

Leaders should also evaluate if there are too many hierarchical layers. Too many layers may cause organizational leaders to be out of touch because they are too far from the frontlines where the mission is directly carried out. Again, context, growth and current needs for the vision should determine the structure.

3. *Structure by aspiration.* A number of years ago I was invited to work with an organization as a board member. Before attending my first meeting, I learned by reading their website and bylaws that they had an executive director, a director of administration, a director of ministry and outreach, a director of development and a director of communications. When I attended my first meeting, I learned there were only three people in the whole organization! Obviously, this was too much structure for such a tiny, new organization.

Organizational structures are often created or changed by copying another organization. That is not necessarily wrong, but it may not be the appropriate structure for the vision, age, stage and context of the organization or team. It is tempting to imitate other organizations' structures because they seemingly have success in their work—a quick fix. Like anything else in organizational life, certain structures may be passing fads.

Leaders who copy another organization's structure or follow a popular fad normally have not evaluated their needs. They expect magical success by patterning themselves after another fruitful ministry. In other words, since this method works in church X, maybe it will resolve our problems and bring similar success in our church. Such a quick fix bypasses the hard work that's needed to understand the deeper issues in the context and evaluate what structural solutions will be best.

4. Structure by *personality phenom*. The personality-driven structure may be the most dangerous of all. In organizations built around one charismatic leader, teams and administration are designed to protect and support this personality phenom. An example is the multisite church where the sermons of one talented preacher are beamed to other satellite locations. The megachurch that grows because of the gifts and personality of one leader is a variation on the same theme.

Dependence on one person and the problem of leadership succession are two obvious challenges inherent in this approach. Is this structure sustainable? What happens when the personality phenom leaves or dies? Or when another personality phenom becomes more popular? And what does one person doing the ministry of the church communicate about who does or does not do ministry? Should not everyone be equipped for the work of ministry as Paul suggests in Ephesians 4:11-13?

These four approaches to structure should be avoided because they tend to hinder evaluation, innovation and adaptation to changing contexts. If your church or team operates with one of these tendencies, it may be time to seriously evaluate the structure to see if (1) it frees and supports people to participate in the mission and (2) it is flexible and adaptive for changing contexts. You might consider a couple of other more desirable structure options.

5. *Structure by function*. As Mintzberg proposes, organizational structure is simply the division and coordination of labor. In chapter eight we asked, What are the activities we need to do our mission and pursue our vision? What are all the functions necessary in our work and what type of coordination is needed for those functions? The answers to these questions give us clues toward structure.

In structuring by function, leaders first regularly assess what activities are essential for doing the mission and moving toward the outcomes of the vision. Second, they assess what activities support the accomplishment of the mission and vision. Third, depending on the outcomes of their assessment, they change or make adjustments to the structure to free energy and support activities that directly connect with the mission and vision.

Analysis like this is key. It helps leaders know whether or not their strategies enable the team to fulfill the mission and vision or if they just repeat programs that they've always done.

The need for structural changes may also be signaled when functions or procedures become too cumbersome. People who encounter processes in the structure for the first time are best suited to evaluate. Those who have been around for a while have gotten used to the inefficiencies and often fail to see them anymore. Therefore, similar to conducting an exit interview, conduct an entrance interview to understand what it is like to encounter a process for the first time.

In a similar manner, whole teams can initiate procedural analyses. By taking time to step back and chart processes in their areas, they may notice repetition, steps that are not needed or points of pain (something that does not work) in the overall process. These may indicate structural problems, and teams can initiate changes to better streamline functions.

6. Structure for synergy. Admittedly, I have rarely seen groups structure for synergy. Yet as I have facilitated a process to introduce this approach in several organizations that are highly compartmentalized or siloed, I have witnessed its power.[3]

World Grace Ministries (WGM) was a thriving organization of around one hundred people, mobilizing Christians to complete the task of world evangelization. Based in Australia, they had nine active departments pursuing this mission:

- *Education*—designing and producing educational materials to raise awareness and involvement in world mission
- *Traveling teams*—coordinating and training missionaries on home assignments to travel

to college campuses to educate and mobilize students for mission
- *Research teams*—conducting ethnographic research among unreached people groups (UPGs)
- *Media*—creating prayer guides and other products for awareness and education regarding UPGs
- *Web*—presenting research from the research teams
- *Church relations*—bringing WGM products and education into the church contexts
- *Marketing*—promoting and selling WGM products
- *Finance/administration*—overseeing operations

Each of these departments had grown around the ideas and initiatives of talented visionaries, and all were functioning well. However, over time, the review, planning and budgeting process for the nine departments became extremely arduous. The result was a four-inch-thick binder that gathered each department's yearly plan—something that was much too difficult to use throughout the year. The leadership team, composed of the directors from all the departments, also noticed subtle but growing competition for resources. So departments had begun to function independently. These attitudes began to have an impact on the overall morale and progress of WGM.

To initiate the structural intervention, the leadership team and full staff gathered in their yearly retreat to review their mission, vision and core values and answer two questions: What is the essence, the core identity of WGM? Why did God call WGM into existence? They eventually categorized all their answers to the two questions into three general areas—prayer, education and mobilization.

As a result of seeing everything WGM did as part of these three areas, the leaders and the board made a bold move. They decided to eliminate *all* nine departments—not the people, but the departments. The compartmentalization had meant that the experience and knowledge of each department didn't help anyone else. What the media team knew wasn't of use to the traveling and research teams. The church relations and media teams knew nothing about the expertise of the research teams. What the traveling teams were learning from college students wasn't made available to media and church relations.

The new structure was simple. A leadership team remained intact, but it was not a representative-government type of leadership team. Rather, they chose people known to have leadership and strategic gifts and asked them to be on the leadership team. They also kept intact an administrative/finance team focused on the operations of the organization. The president was a member of both teams to provide consistency between strategy and operations. These were the only two permanent teams. Otherwise, staff representing multiple disciplines came together in ad hoc teams to work on projects related to education, prayer and mobilization. When the project was complete, the ad hoc team disbanded and a new team was formed to start a new project. No more silos. No more protecting turf. The wisdom, disciplines and knowledge of multiple people synergized to move the mission forward, beyond what the individual departments could accomplish on their own.

What happened to the entrepreneurial directors of the former departments? As you might guess, the proposal to eliminate all the departments was extremely threatening, and the directors of the former departments essentially lost their position. They were used to their relatively autonomous domain and the presumed security of having a title. Much of their leadership was redirected toward managing ad hoc project teams that formed and disbanded as needed. Egos had to remain in check with an overall selfless posture toward seeing the vision accomplished. Not easy for us human beings!

Yet the miracle and joy of creating an environment where true collaboration leads to achieving something beyond anyone's own abilities was truly fulfilling. As they experienced the energy released when uniquely gifted people offered their expertise on one project, the excitement and fruitfulness was extremely satisfying. They could see increased movement toward doing the mission and accomplishing the vision.

The purpose of structuring for synergy is to free expertise, knowledge and experiences that are normally dedicated to one area (say, a department) for the sake of the whole organization. Doing this normally means dissolving some departments or sectors that have become siloed. This type of structuring brings individual parts to bear on the whole.

There is loss, however. People may have their identities as part of a department. They may miss not working closely with those who have become good friends. They may be defensive about having to learn how to do their work differently or by learning something entirely new. Leaders can be threatened by the loss of power or prestige. Restructuring for synergy may demand a lot for any organization. Those most affected may need a lot of one-on-one time from leaders to help them process the changes and get the reassurance they need that they are still valued members of the team. Leaders will need to acknowledge openly that this change, no matter how good it is, still means loss for some. They will be wise to lead their teams in celebrating and thanking God for the past, even as they can move forward.

You likely noticed that structuring for synergy can be a more fluid approach to organizational structures. Normally, structures are formed by dividing people into seemingly logical categories or areas—for example, those focused on literature in one department, those focused on adult ministries in another department, those focused on children's ministries in another department, those focused on outreach in another department and so on. Yet this method may prevent collaboration leading to fruitful outcomes, especially in older organizations where there may be turf-protecting tactics and competition for resources. In these situations, the survival of the department can become more important than the mission of the organization (although, of course, no one would admit that).

When structuring for synergy, the core mission is reaffirmed—beyond all departments, activities, projects and programs—and pursued with the expertise, experience and gifts of everyone in the organization. Similar to the process of pruning and grafting a vine, the elimination of redundancy and combining of the compartments produces synergy, leading to breakthroughs and outcomes never before imagined. This is flourishing.

12
THE NUTS AND BOLTS OF STRUCTURE

Organizations tend to fall into structures rather than think deliberately about them. As mentioned in chapter eleven, we are likely to structure ourselves by tradition, by a chart, by aspiration or by personality. In this chapter I want us to consider how we can go about deliberately thinking about structure rather than just inheriting it.

ELEMENTS OF STRUCTURE

Based on Henry Mintzberg's research regarding structure, there are four elements necessary for the proper functioning of any organization.[1] These elements should be included, in varying strength, when designing structure. Note: the elements may or may not be actual people or divisions or departments. That is not the focus. The critical factor is that the elements must be present for the organization to flourish. How they exist, whether embodied in people or in the goals of a department, depends on what is appropriate for the mission, vision, age and stage of the organization. Here they are.

1. Leadership. Two aspects of leadership are needed. First, there must be accountability to the mission, vision and values of the organization. An entity or body must ensure that the organization stays true to the reason for which it exists. People need to be held accountable to accomplish certain goals. The accountability may be to a group like a board or leadership team, or through individuals. Second, leaders need to make sure the mission, vision and values are translated to all parts of the organization. This could be through people, such as managers, coaches or small group leaders, or it could be through training processes or some type of standardized requirements.

2. Direct ministers. Every organization has a frontline that carries out the essential activities of the mission and vision. Without them the core mission would not be accomplished. In a church this would be everyone who identifies themselves as followers of Jesus and who are committed to their community. In a campus ministry, they are the workers who evangelize, disciple and equip students. In a church-planting mission agency, they are ministers endeavoring to start new communities of faith.

3. Support. Operations like finance, personnel, technology and the like free those in direct ministry and leadership to do their work effectively. Like a vine lacking a post and wire so that the fruit is dragging on the ground, under-supported organizations find it difficult to flourish.

4. *Catalysts*. The status quo must always be challenged. Despite the discomfort that may ensue, organizations need people or processes that press everyone into asking, How can we do our work better? More efficiently? Are we closer to accomplishing our vision? Challenging the status quo can create a lot of conflict and tension. Such people must, therefore, be deeply immersed in the DNA. If not, such challenges can take an organization or team down a dead end. But if done in a way that respects the culture, respects people and respects the vision, they can equip members and the team to constantly grow and develop. This is the catalyst function.

In my observation, the catalyst function is most often missing. Think about it. What could be more crucial for announcing, demonstrating and living in the kingdom of God than asking how we can do this better or more effectively? The very essence of transformation requires that these questions are researched and pursued. Yet I find resistance to asking, How can we do it better? For some, the question seems unspiritual. "We just need to be faithful to our work and the Spirit will do the rest." Not untrue! But I imagine there may be smarter and more innovative ways to do "our work." For others, contentment with and commitment to the same programs year after year preclude big-picture evaluation.

In addition, if leaders and members are operating with a general sense of fatigue, asking how to do things better requires too much energy. Therefore, they stay with the status quo. This is sad, because people's lives may depend on our doing strategies, methods, programs, activities, operations and trainings more effectively and efficiently each year.

Again, the four elements of structure may be embodied in people, processes or systems, but they must be present for an organization to flourish and be sustainable over time. Returning to our metaphor of the grapevine, the vine will naturally sprout, blossom and produce fruit according to its DNA. Therefore, we must select and reproduce the organizational DNA in those who carry out the ministry—*direct*. This requires that leaders live and inculcate the mission, vision and values—*leadership*. For the vine to live off the ground and capture more sun, it needs the support of stakes and wire. Support releases the vine to flourish by allowing it to grow and spread out and making it more available to the sun. *Support* structures in organizations do the same by channeling energy and resources. Adding water and nutrients increases fruit on the vine, just as providing care and training increases flourishing—*catalysts*. Finally, pruning eliminates branches that will not bear fruit and gives fruitful branches more access to the sun resulting in more fruit. Eliminating waste or redundancy and implementing more effective strategies can create energy and produce better results—also *catalysts*.

At this point in your reflection, it might be helpful to evaluate the strength of the four elements of structure for your organization. Review the elements, and then draw a diagram that illustrates their relative strength and presence in your context.

A symbolic diagram is one way to picture how the different elements of structure might look in an organization. It shows the relative size of the different groups and how they overlap. Figure 12.1 offers an example of an organization I'll call Water for the World Ministries. What insights might you gain from this diagram?

In figure 12.1, the catalysts circle is small, practically nonexistent, especially in comparison to those in direct ministry. The catalyst structure has no overlap with leadership, which may indicate that there is little overall quest for innovation and increasing effectiveness. In fact, those who challenge the status quo may find themselves isolated or voiceless. The long-term effects of this scenario most likely lead to languishing rather than flourishing.

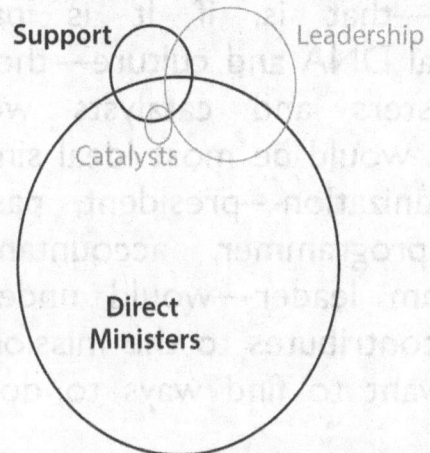

Figure 12.1. Elements of structure in Water for the World Ministries

> ### Stop and Think
> Draw a diagram of the four elements of structure for your organization or team. Show overlap and relative size of each element.
> • What do you learn from your diagram?
> • Where are you strongest and weakest? Why?
>
> If you are in a group, have each individual draw their diagrams independently and then discuss.
> • What are similarities and differences?
> • Why do you think people have different perspectives?

A final comment on the elements of structure: if the quest for doing work better, more effectively, exists in each person in the organization—that is, if it is part of the organizational DNA and culture—then circles for direct ministers and catalysts would totally overlap. This would be most ideal since everyone in the organization—president, pastor, janitor, computer programmer, accountant, program director, team leader—would understand how their work contributes to the mission and would constantly want to find ways to do their work better.

BEST PRACTICES—STRUCTURE

Over the years I've found a number of ideas to be especially fruitful when it comes to structure. Let me highlight a few.

No representative governance. In chapter eleven we met WGM, who took the radical step of disbanding all its departments. They disbanded their representative structure almost entirely. This may seem odd or even scandalous for those of us living in democratically led countries. Ideally, however, leadership teams should consist of men and women who have leadership qualities—creativity, leading, exhorting, strategizing, visioning—and who are absolutely committed to working together and serving and enabling others toward the fulfillment of the vision.

Most organizations I encounter structure their leadership team like WGM did, in a representative way. In a church, one person might represent women, another children, another seniors, another adults, another administration and so on. The mandate and expectation for each of these leaders is to represent—argue for—their constituency. Each views potential programs, activities and finances through the lens of how they will impact those they represent.

The problems with this methodology are threefold. First, the priority of the "good" of the constituency displaces the overall good of the organization. For the representatives, the good of their own group is first and foremost in their minds. This leads to compromising give-and-take, and often, decisions are reached and implemented at the lowest common denominator.

Second, the leadership team may or may not be composed of people who actually have gifts related to leadership. If their job description is to represent people like them and that is the primary qualification, they may not possess actual experience and gifts in leadership. This makes it difficult, if not impossible, for the leadership team to function in strategic, visionary endeavors.

Third, the loudest voice or the squeaky wheel wins. Inevitably one constituency is deemed more important than others—we know this because decisions are most often taken in their favor—yet their importance makes no logical sense. Perhaps it is because the representative contributes the most money. Or perhaps decisions favor the representative who complains the most because their complaining exhausts the rest of the team, so they give in. Whatever the case, a few dominate the others, and the vision of the organization is lost.

Perhaps this is obvious, but for this "nonrepresentative government" concept, I do make a distinction between leadership teams and boards. Leadership teams and boards are similar in that they both ensure accountability to the mission, vision and values. Yet leadership teams also oversee those who are directly doing the work of the organization, as well as operations. For the makeup of the board, ideally a wide variety of experiences and expertise should be sought. Not so that constituencies can be represented, but so that diverse experiences related to the vision can be offered.

Let me also add that it is absolutely critical for leaders to hear and know the diverse voices in their organization. This can be accomplished in a wide variety of ways besides instituting representative governance. Max De Pree is an exemplar of the listening leader. He would invite anyone in the company, twenty at a time, to have lunch with him and the senior management once a month.[2] During this time, workers were invited to ask questions and offer ideas. Their ideas often initiated changes that truly helped the company function better. Max also regularly visited the factory floor and talked with line managers and those working in the production line. In this fashion he stayed in touch with their work and created an atmosphere of trust and care.

Separate strategy and operations. Something else we saw at WGM in chapter eleven was separating strategic and operational functions. Operational functions are those regular tasks for which there is already an agreed upon system, such as procedures related to finances, human resources, facilities management, etc. I recommend placing these functions, including policy development, within an operations team rather than in a strategic leadership team.

Operational concerns have a tendency to become urgent and time-consuming and then take precedence over strategic issues, such as creative envisioning and planning for the future, program evaluation and consideration of new opportunities. It is easy for leadership teams to spend most of their time discussing money and what color to paint the office rather than doing the high-level analysis required for the vision to be accomplished.

Stop and Think

Take a look at the agenda and minutes of one of your recent leadership team meetings.
- What percentage of the meetings incorporates administrative or operational functions and what percentage focuses on high-level strategic issues?
- Which items will significantly help advance mission?

> • Is there a way to delegate some or all of these operational issues to another team? If so, how?

Please hear the distinction I am making. I am not saying that operational issues are unimportant or unsupportive of the vision. It is critical that finance systems be run efficiently. Donors must be thanked in a timely fashion. Checks and balances must be in place to maintain integrity and accountability. Efficient procedures for mobilizing and orienting people who join the organization are essential. However, when good systems are in place, they should not be agenda items on the strategic leadership team but rather entrusted to the process and people who are responsible.

Recognize that structuring leadership depends on the size and mission of the organization. If an organization has a leadership team focused on mission and strategy and another focused on operations, how can you ensure effective communication? One option is for several people to belong to both teams. Another is to have a joint meeting once per quarter.

Another possibility is to have one team with both types of leaders, operational and strategic. But the group would then need to discipline itself to structure agendas to focus on one area or the other—not both operations and strategy in the same meeting. Assuming operations are running smoothly, the team could focus on this aspect once a month for a designated period of time, say one hour. Normally strategic focus needs more time. Research needs to be assigned, carried out and presented; opportunities evaluated and breakthrough ideas pursued. Minimally speaking, strategy-focused sessions should be allotted two days per quarter.[3]

A lot of leadership teams function around reports or report giving. This is a colossal waste of time. People can read reports and must discipline themselves to do so. When the team is together, it is time for synergistic work that advances the mission, not giving reports.

Ensure scalability and sustainability. When considering structural change, we should ask if the new arrangement is scalable to include more people and grow with the organization. At what point would it become unwieldy and unsustainable? When would it be too difficult to employ because of too many layers for effective communication or the pursuit of opportunities?

If leaders anticipate the future and the point at which the structure will need to be evaluated and changed again, they can help members realize that no structure is permanent. Leaders can communicate that there will come a time down the road when it will need to change again. This helps people become more comfortable with restructuring because they see it as part of the normal cycle of the life of the organization.

LAST BUT NOT LEAST

Here are a few final reminders. The first one won't surprise you.

*1. **Structure must flow from the organization's mission and vision and embody the core values.*** Conversations about structure or structural change should always be in reference to the mission, vision and values. We need to ask,

- Is our structure helping or hindering those who do the mission and accomplish our vision, and how?
- How does our structure make our values reality or not?
- How can we see our values operating in the structure?

*2. **Regular evaluation of the structure enables leaders to discern whether or not it is helping the organization connect with and adapt to its context.*** Loss of connection to the environment due to too many structural layers may cause the organization to become irrelevant to the target of their vision. Key questions are,

- How can we connect better?
- How can we do our mission better?
- In what ways is our structure cumbersome or redundant?
- Is our structure scalable?

- How will we need to change the structure as we grow?

3. *Keep it simple*—and if not simple, at least keep it appropriate for the age, stage and goals of the organization. In the early stages of organization growth, very little structure is needed. People share jobs, perhaps even rotating who does payroll, sets up chairs, preaches, cleans the office and so forth. Over time, more division of labor is appropriate, because professional expertise in, for example, finance, technology or human resources is needed. One must ensure, however, that the division of labor does not promote walled compartmentalization, which potentially leads to turf wars and competition for resources.

Most organizational structures evolve in a variety of ways as we saw in chapter eleven. By keeping the principles and elements of structure in mind, we can keep that growth from being haphazard. We can intentionally create structures that serve our staff and our constituency so that both they and the organization flourish.

13

THE FUTURE OF FLOURISHING—INNOVATION AND ENTREPRENEURS

A survey of the last two thousand years of church history reveals that movements of God often begin on the fringes or periphery of the established church. In fact, Paul Pierson, former dean of the School of World Mission at Fuller, documents this phenomenon in his book *The Dynamics of Christian Mission.*[1] Even the first-century Jesus movement was unable to begin in the central religious establishment of the Pharisees, chief priests and teachers of the Law; rather, it began through a ragtag community of Spirit-empowered men and women following their Lord's call and commands, eventually leading to gatherings in homes, outside synagogues and temples.

The problem is that over time, these new vital movements tend to institutionalize and become unresponsive to God's interventions and the world around them. I once asked Dr. Pierson if there was a way to prevent this trend. Is there a way to keep a movement a movement, vital and flexible, once it has become established or is in its third, fourth or fifth generation? He thought for a while and then replied, "Movements can remain movements as long as the fringe remains—as long as creative impetus is woven into the fabric of the movement." That was hopeful.

Ichak Adizes shows that organizations "age" when they become rigid, inflexible and unable to respond to changing contexts. For Adizes's "life-cycles of organizations" theory, decreasing innovation—leading to the absence of entrepreneurialism—signals movement toward aging and the eventual death of the organization; thus, pronounced entrepreneurialism signals sustainability and life—flourishing. Aging occurs when there is a lack of entrepreneurialism and organizations become highly administrative (bureaucratic) and inward focused, so that energy distribution is directed toward its own survival rather than doing the mission and fulfilling the vision.[2]

Visionary companies (that is, flourishing organizations) manifest a constant drive for progress—"a deep human urge—to explore, to create, to discover, to achieve, to change, to improve."[3] So how can we think and act intentionally about entrepreneurialism, the future of flourishing in our organizations?

IT'S THE PEOPLE!

Maintaining an entrepreneurial edge in organizations requires (1) cultivating entrepreneurs and (2) cultivating an environment, an organization, where entrepreneurs thrive. Let me address the people aspect first.

Reaching People was not an old mission agency, but it had recently instituted professional management systems for mobilization and finance. The personnel department conducted the DiSC assessment (a nonjudgmental personality profile) for all new workers.[4] As I consulted with Reaching People, we looked at several years of DiSC profiles and noticed that 95 percent of men and women who joined were either high Ss (steadiness) or Cs (conscientious or compliant). In other words, the primary personality bent of most new hires were those who thrive in environments where there is not a lot of change—steady—and where there are well-established rules and procedures—compliant. Yet the organization's vision focused on pioneering new work in challenging, developing-world contexts.

We also discovered that those who recruited and oversaw the candidate processes were also high Ss and Cs (not surprising since managers of procedures often are and need to be high Ss and Cs!). Unknowingly, the "like-attracts-like" principle was operating, and entrepreneurs either self-selected out of the mobilization process, because they were not attracted to the Ss and Cs, or the high Ss and Cs unwittingly discouraged entrepreneurs from applying. (An aside regarding personality profiles: obviously personality is only one aspect of a person's being. Giftedness—including natural abilities, acquired skills and spiritual gifts—and one's spiritual pilgrimage are other aspects. Therefore, it is conceivable that a person could be a high C and have the spiritual gift of apostleship; in other words, he or she is spiritually an entrepreneur.)

When we reviewed the application and interview questions, they did a solid job of asking applicants to describe their spiritual journeys, including their spiritual gifts. But questions related to leadership, creativity, starting new ventures and thriving in challenging situations were noticeably absent. The managers, along with the process, almost made it impossible to identify entrepreneurs who might join the organization!

What could Reaching People have done? Here are some ideas: (1) find ways to highlight the entrepreneurs in the organization and let them tell their stories through various media and mobilizing events; (2) change initial information and application forms to include questions that sought and revealed those with proven entrepreneurial experiences; (3) streamline the application process (without compromising quality), because entrepreneurs can be notoriously impatient with such formalities; and (4) train and equip managers to know and understand the heart and motivation of an entrepreneur so they can appreciate the difference and gifts in this personality type. This can enable them to suspend judgment when they encounter personalities different from their own.

Assuming kingdom-of-God organizations are compelled to grow, reproduce and flourish until their God-given vision is accomplished—or until Jesus Christ returns—it is absolutely necessary to attract and nurture entrepreneurs. And yet entrepreneurs are a somewhat peculiar breed—always challenging the status quo, noticing gaps when things are not perfect, suggesting how to improve everything they encounter. They are impatient with rules, procedures, "the way we have always done it" and the word *no*. Placing entrepreneurs in situations that require them to monitor and maintain a program is a recipe for disaster. They will either die on the vine or create chaos so they have something to fix. Perfectly efficient and beneficial systems become unwieldy with an entrepreneur's touch. Ensure, then, that once entrepreneurs join the organization, they direct their catalytic energies toward opportunities and innovations that advance the mission.

Stop and Think

Briefly jot down responses to the following:

> - Who are the entrepreneurs in your department, team or organization (those who like to start new ventures, engage new groups of customers, think up new processes and so forth)?
> - What is done to encourage them and give them space to operate or test new ideas?

Beyond cultivating entrepreneurs, how do you cultivate a culture that can attract, release and nurture entrepreneurialism? Ensuring that entrepreneurialism is a vital life force in the organization must be a priority focus for organization development efforts. The entrepreneurial spirit is the key factor for enabling the creativity and innovation needed to respond to constantly changing contexts and continue the mission. In the following sections, I revisit organizational culture and structures as they relate to creating space for entrepreneurialism.

THE ENTREPRENEURIAL CULTURE

My first encounter with Prison Fellowship International's leadership team startled me—loud voices, open disagreements, interruptions, debate, pacing and random drawing on the white board. I silently observed. Having just come from a predominantly Asian context where much of the creative impetus happens outside the formal meeting, the obvious energy in the room intrigued but scared me. The strategy session seemed more like a boisterous family dinner than an executive leadership team meeting. Yet, as I continued to listen and notice the building momentum, I discovered that with each proposed idea, each disagreement, each counter idea, there was a repeated sense of cohesion. The proposal, in this free-flowing, seemingly meandering process, became something new and more likely to succeed.

I had read and taught Pat Lencioni's *Five Dysfunctions of a Team* for years, but this was the first time I encountered his principles lived out in an organization's executive team.[5] This team had obviously overcome the barriers of lack of trust and fear of conflict.

Flourishing organizational cultures promote entrepreneurialism, because flourishing assumes newness, growth, creativity and innovation. When people flourish, their brains automatically create and broaden the number of opportunities or avenues available to pursue, whereas controlling or fearful environments curtail creativity and narrow options. Let's consider the characteristics of an organizational culture that nurtures entrepreneurs.

First, the culture is safe. All people express their gifts and ideas in a free-flowing way full of conflicting ideas as well as synergistic scenarios. Shared ideas, created in dialogue and collaboration, build on each other so that the best solutions emerge. A buzz, a life-giving pulse, characterizes the meeting as all contribute their unique perspectives. No one holds back. Everyone's voice is valid, welcomed and needed. Synergistic strategies result from the collaboration of voices.

Second, the creative process produces results exponentially beyond what individuals could offer or are able to do. The combination of individual ideas and experiences coalesce into new, never-before-thought-of solutions. This synergistic impetus becomes the trusted norm, and therefore individual egos submit to serve the greater, next idea. This aspect, at times, feels supernatural, as the collective manifestation of the Spirit of God creates. Teams invent strategies, programs and activities beyond previously imagined methods.

Third, one senses the absolute sheer delight of learning. First experienced in childhood and sometimes squelched in educational systems, the joy of learning is recovered in flourishing environments. Of course the delight of learning assumes humility. We know our gaps and weaknesses—and so does everyone else! And that's okay, because we can learn! God entrusts us with an unlimited capacity and possibility to change, to transform. Keep in mind, however, that we do not have to learn it all ourselves, because flourishing cultures are interdependent communities. Other members of our teams or others in the organization have wisdom and gifts.

We can endeavor to affirm others' strengths and protect their weaknesses.[6]

Fourth, following from learning, there must be a rhythm of reflection. It is nearly impossible for frazzled, frenetic people to learn or create. We can learn from intense, challenging periods of work—these seasons often provide the most fruit for learning. But in order to learn and create out of these intense periods, we must have space for reflection. Therefore, I have found it helpful (and this ties into the following section on structures) to bring teams away on retreat—with no smartphones, iPads or computers. The purpose is to interactively reflect on our work and ask questions such as, What is going well? What is not going well? In an overall sense, what would make our work better? What seems impossible to do today, but if it were possible would have a radical impact on accomplishing the vision?

I have also asked—or required, depending on the circumstances—that employees set aside 10 percent of their time or one week per quarter to think about their work and participate in something creative (go to an art museum, take a walk in nature, write poetry, draw, paint—even finger paint—etc.). Creative encounters free the mind to think differently, which also opens us to new ideas or ways of accomplishing our work. We then meet in teams to capture ideas or resystematize processes we discovered are not working well.

Safety, ideas, learning (from others' and our own organization's innovations), experimenting and risk taking characterize an organizational culture where entrepreneurialism thrives. These cultures are able to innovate and adapt to the rapidly changing global context and thus stay on task for their mission and on target for their vision.

ENTREPRENEURIAL STRUCTURES

Besides cultivating entrepreneurs and environments where entrepreneurs flourish, structures and structural interventions support entrepreneurialism as well. Here are a few ideas.

1. Put your money where your mouth is! Innovations proceed from research and experimentation. As a practice each year, require budget managers to set aside a portion of revenues for new ventures or startups based on research and understanding of the context. Ideas and proposals submitted to the leadership or an appointed committee could be entertained with the most appropriate proposal (for advancing the mission) receiving startup funds. Spinning off reproducing teams or churches or new projects has the overall effect of "youth-inizing" the whole organization, even aspects of it that seem old.

OMF International's work in Thailand experienced a lift through a process like this.

Missionaries in Northern Thailand wanted to minister across borders in countries such as Myanmar, China, Vietnam and Laos, where traditional missions and missionary visas were not permitted. Yet the rest of the Thailand field focused on the Thai people, and their operation was fully accepted by the Thai government, which issued their missionary visas. Because of the intense difference in these two foci and their required strategic methodologies (missionary visas versus professional visas), the leaders in the Thailand field decided to release those in Northern Thailand who wanted to serve people groups in the traditionally closed countries. The existing Thailand and Mekong field was divided, and the new field developed different supportive structures, which soon grew to be even larger than the rest of the Thailand field. Innovative, creative ministries emerged that connected with people in Myanmar, China, Vietnam and Laos. The growth of this field and the stories of God's work among people in these locations had the overall effect of encouraging the Thailand field and the rest of the organization, along with promoting the possibility of new ventures in other countries. In this way the organizational aging process was slowed and even reversed.

2. Research and design (R&D). Just as commercial enterprises have teams focused on R & D, churches and Christian organizations can do the same. An R & D group constantly learns, attends to global realities, stays attentive to creative developments in other contexts and brainstorms how all these realities might create opportunities for growing the organization. This can be a truly synergistic process, because unassociated, unexpected disciplines, such as those related to science or technology, may be synthesized in order to create never-before-thought-of innovations.

Understandably, few nonprofit organizations can afford the luxury of fully dedicated research teams, but every organization has R & D–type people who could gather on an ad hoc basis for specific issues that need attention and energy for advancement. This leads us to the next idea.

3. Breakthrough gatherings. Let's say an organization has been unable to grow or reproduce. Various initiatives have been tried to no avail. The purpose of a breakthrough gathering is to bring together diverse people, from every part of the organization, to research, imagine and propose pilot projects that have potential to catalyze growth. Pilot projects are then selected and implemented with regular monitoring and evaluation. Reflecting on and learning from the pilot project leads to the potential for application and implementation in other parts of the organization. A small team that has the vision and passion for the project can accomplish this.

The gatherings should be regular yet ad hoc in their makeup. Regular, because in any organization there is always need for breakthroughs of some type, not just those related to growth. Sometimes there are challenges or blockages that need fresh eyes and study in order to attempt breakthrough. Ad hoc, because wider and diverse participation will more likely bring fresh possibilities and solutions. Communities of practice may facilitate breakthroughs as well, and that is next.

4. *Communities of practice.* While communities of practice have existed for millennia (such as apprenticeships for artisans, metalworkers, masons, potters, etc.), promoting their existence in organizations enables sharing of knowledge and best practices, especially in an age when technological breakthroughs come often and at lightening speed. Communities of practice are "groups of people informally bound together by shared expertise and passion for a joint enterprise."[7] They may meet over lunch, around coffee, via email or the Internet, but essentially individual disciplines are offered to, for example, improve processes, create new strategy or increase efficiency in operational functions. Communities of practice ask: How can we do our work better? How can we apply a technological advancement to our strategies? And so on.

Individuals who have mastered certain disciplines, say accountancy or human resource laws, may not be entrepreneurs themselves. Yet sharing ideas in gatherings with others from their discipline sparks other ideas, and soon discoveries lead to innovation, which has the overall effect of increasing entrepreneurialism.

Structurally speaking, communities of practice should be informal and organic. Too much structure squelches the flow of creativity, so really, the formation of the groupings is focused more on relationships, bringing together the right people to converse or address a challenge. This brings us to the next type of gathering.

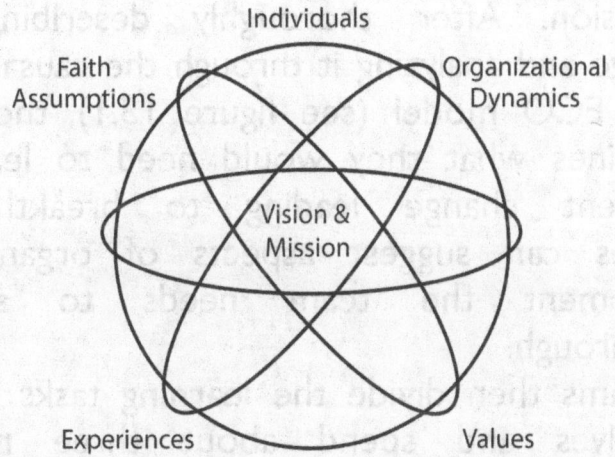

Figure 13.1. The Ecology of Organizations (ECO) model

5. Action-learning projects. Because leaders' schedules are full, leadership teams must structure learning. Adopting an action-learning project is one way for teams to structure learning, which will then release entrepreneurialism. Used in educational programs such as MIT's Sloan School of Management, action learning is an organization development approach in which teams address real-life, organizational challenges that hamper results. Through facilitated, structured questions, usually from a coach, the team reflects on as many aspects of the challenge as possible and then acts or experiments to implement in order to address the challenge. After the action, the team engages in more questioning and learning and then acts again.[8] This think-act-reflect cycle is repeated until change results.

Each team can begin by choosing a significant project for or ongoing barrier to accomplishing the vision. After thoroughly describing the challenge and analyzing it through the causal loops of the ECO model (see figure 13.1), the team determines what they would need to learn to implement change leading to breakthrough. Coaches can suggest aspects of organization development the team needs to see a breakthrough.

Teams then divide the learning tasks among themselves and spend about three months learning. Reconvening again, all members share what they have learned and how this applies to the organizational challenge. After more reflection and questioning, the team synthesizes their learning and brings it to bear on a change strategy for the challenge. The change strategy is then written and implemented.

Ninety percent of the teams I've helped saw significant breakthroughs in challenges that had plagued their organizations for years. Another way to describe the steps of such a group can be found in table 13.1.

Structured learning through action-learning projects uncovers entrepreneurial ideas that have the potential for breakthrough impact. The discipline of learning is most effective in the accountability of a team. Examples of initiatives from such teams often relate to creative structures, leadership formation, capacity development, web-based mobilization, global strategy development, high-impact volunteers and globalization.

6. Protect the entrepreneurs. As a church or organization grows, leaders must standardize and systematize repetitive procedures and incorporate professional management. The organization is not sustainable with the sheer energy of catalytic entrepreneurs and those who do the work of the mission. However, operational procedures, facilities management and finance systems may dampen entrepreneurial zeal. And let's face it, typically, entrepreneurs are impatient with procedures, and managers are exasperated with entrepreneurs. Yet both are absolutely necessary for the longevity and flourishing of the organization. Negotiating the awkwardness between entrepreneurs and administrators requires the correct emphasis on one or the other at the appropriate time, and leaders who respect both.

Table 13.1. Steps for an action-learning project team

Step 1—The story. Begin by telling the story of the challenge as descriptively as possible—its history, the attempted solutions and the results of these solutions—and apply the ECO (Ecology of Organizations) cause-effect loops to trace connections and inner-relationships. The story process will expose organizational leaders' interventions, along with their resulting dynamics and effects on other aspects of the organization. This may reveal leverage in other cause-effect loops, but more likely, since the interventions have not worked, it reveals required areas of study or discipline in order to access true breakthrough.

Step 2—Learning. Based on the analysis thus far and perhaps with coaching from a consultant, team members determine what knowledge or discipline or experience enables them to understand the various factors related to the challenge. Team members then decide who will learn what and set a time to come back together.

Step 3—Reporting. Team members report back what they've learned to the whole team and propose ideas for how the new knowledge connects with the challenge. How might this knowledge offer solutions to change circumstances?

Step 4—Hypotheses. The team then synthesizes these reports to propose possible solutions, experiments, interventions or projects to address the challenge, perhaps transforming it into an entrepreneurial opportunity. Before a plan is designed, however, the team revisits the ECO model and observes all the cause-effect loop connections of the solution. These observations may highlight more possibilities and reveal unexpected consequences.

Step 5—Change plan. Finally, the team initiates a plan with measurable outcomes by identifying the characteristics of breakthrough. They write the change plan and proceed to implement the plan. The plan includes time frames for review, evaluation and amendments as needed. The team envisions success and how the change plan will be scaled in order to impact other parts of the organization.

When it's time to implement professional management, activities directly related to the output of the mission must be slowed—not an easy task, since usually this stage of growth is wildly fruitful. Who wants to slow down when there's growth and success? Yet that is exactly what is needed in order to direct energy toward management systems. However, even though production is slowed, entrepreneurialism must remain strong and even grow. This will ensure that the organization does not prematurely age due to the rigidity of management procedures. Creativity, innovation and new projects must be created and tested so that when mission-related activities come back online, they are given a boost.

> ### Stop and Think
>
> Take a minute and write down possible action-learning projects for your department, team or organization.
>
> Now write down what would be the next steps you would take to have these discussed by those in a position to authorize such teams.

In the midst of creating professional management, leaders must also celebrate and protect the entrepreneurs, sometimes even providing a buffer between the two very different goals. Ultimately, however, as the natural process of institutionalization happens over time, entrepreneurs are likely to leave, especially if they continually hit administrative brick walls; therefore, leaders need to increase their efforts to protect the entrepreneurs and create nurturing venues for their creativity. Here are some ideas for doing just that:

- Keep track of the entrepreneurs in your organization, and whenever possible, assign supervisors who understand their drive and know how to harness their energy. If possible, match them with other more experienced entrepreneurs who can coach and sponsor them. Sometimes entrepreneurs can be hard driving and uncompromising, especially if they also have prophetic gifts. Coaches can advise as to what the entrepreneurs need to do behaviorally speaking (that is, help them grow in emotional intelligence) to make their personalities more palatable and less demanding.

- Initiate once-yearly entrepreneurial gatherings where organizational leaders share future growth goals and interact together with the entrepreneurs for innovations toward these goals. Provide space also for the entrepreneurs to share their best ideas or practices from the past year. This practice could be initiated in the gathering and continued via the web. In general, create an open-source ethos for all ideas and best practices.
- Create training for the entrepreneurs in such areas as emotional intelligence, leadership succession, obtaining funding, writing grant proposals, project management, sustainability and so forth. This will increase their ability to bring good ideas into reality.

Cultivating entrepreneurs and an entrepreneurial environment are absolutely essential for the organization's growth and sustainability. In a flourishing organism, innovation is the most natural thing. But in organizations, because they are prone to institutionalization, staying entrepreneurial requires intentional focus and discipline. Entrepreneurs must be attracted, nurtured and released in the context of a well-run, efficient organization. Not an easy task.

14

FLOURISHING: A DAILY REALITY

Several of my courses typically include students who are pastors. Often I ask about the activities their churches are engaged in. Not surprising, the list comprises Sunday school, adult Bible studies, children's programs, small groups, a yearly Alpha course, baptism class, feeding the homeless, choir, worship band, yearly mission trips and so on.

Typically, I also ask about each church's sense of mission and vision. What has God called their faith community to do or accomplish? While the pastors can list their programs and what they do on a weekly basis, they usually have more trouble with what the church's sense is of the results God has called them to accomplish. Why has God formed and called their faith community into existence?

Some were able to pull up mission and vision statements from their websites, but the statements were not familiar to the pastors. Also, the statements did not describe the pastors' reasons for being or what they thought God had called them to accomplish. Probing further, I asked the pastors why they do the various programs they do. Most responses could be categorized as, "That's what we have always done," "That's what we notice other churches doing," or more frighteningly, "That's what church is."

I have lived and worked in a context where the church is rapidly growing (East and Southeast Asia), been immersed in a multinational team and organization, and had a job description primarily focused on developing and training church planters. This has given me the gift of ample opportunities to explore the question, What is church, really? And while ecclesiology is not the topic of this book, my experience of church in these contexts led me to the realization that most of the time we do "church" activities and programs without any real discernment about the unique calling and essence of our faith communities for their particular context.

We do programs because we have always done them or because they work in other churches or because they have come to define what church is. It is not that the programs themselves are wrong or bad, and they may even be appropriate. It's just that often we have not done the prayerful, faith-filled, hard work of imagining God's future for our context and our called community.

Up to this point in the book, we have been working with the big-picture concepts of mission, vision, values, faith assumptions, organizational culture, structures and so forth. Now I bring the perspective to ground level and demonstrate how mission and vision translate into strategies, daily practices and goals in the trenches.

> ### Stop and Think
> Ask in your context: If we, by God's enabling grace, accomplish what God has given us to accomplish, what will we see? Be as specific as you can.

Prayer-filled envisioning of the future in a participative process results in God's picture of the future for your context. It is critical to describe this picture in as much imaginative detail as possible, because this detail points toward what should be done in the present to get to the future. Here are some steps a group can take toward strategy development.

1. Future-perfect imagining. In as much detail as possible and with as many people as possible, describe your context as if the vision has already happened.
- What will you see?
- What will you feel?
- What will you notice about relationships?
- What differences will you see in the community because of God's kingdom reign?
- How will things be transformed?
- How will you know the kingdom of God is present?

- What is the situation now and how will it be different if your community partners with God to accomplish kingdom-oriented outcomes?

In a whole or focus-group(s) process, capture on paper or on a projector the pictures people describe. Notice and pay particular attention to descriptions that increase energy and excitement in the flow of conversation and offerings. These signal important articulations of the vision that engage, compel and bring a sense of urgency. They inspire faith and will enable powerful communication, which will in turn draw others into the vision.

2. Isolate and describe general categories. When this participatory process seems saturated (new pictures offered repeat what has previously been offered), have the group isolate and describe the general categories of the vision. These are the God-inspired results or outcomes. You may then find it helpful to have several people start with the vision statement and write a one-page description/exegesis of the vision that incorporates the general categories of results—what will be seen when the vision comes into being.

3. Back from the future. Once the vision has been imagined as if it has already happened, take a step back in time, toward the present, and imagine the context just before the vision

is accomplished. Conduct the end-visioning process described in chapter eight.
- What will you see, feel and know in the environment/context?
- What will already be in place?
- What will need to be instigated in order for the vision to be fully accomplished?

Describing the circumstances just before the vision is accomplished enables you to check whether the picture, the outcomes of the vision, has been adequately described. If adjustments need to be made in the exegesis, go ahead and make them at this point. Thoroughness in this envisioning process promotes effective strategy development.

At this point, teams may find it helpful to take a few more descriptive steps back in time toward the present so that they more thoroughly understand by what means they will get to the future (see figure 14.1). Of course this can be an arduous exercise, but it saves the organization from investing in programs just for programs' sake and prevents organizational leaders from overlooking key strategies and factors that need to be in place to accomplish the vision.

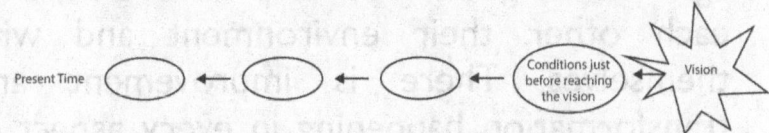

Figure 14.1. Strategy development

Ultimately working toward God's vision for the future means we have to do something in the present! Future-perfect imagining and back-from-the-future exercises ignite faith and uncover possible means to accomplish the vision. Further analysis of the context will reveal key strategies to move the mission forward toward the vision.

You may have noted that I have said very little about context up to this point. That is not because I view context as unimportant. It is absolutely important, because God calls us to incarnate his presence in very specific contexts, and he cares about the distinctives of those contexts. I have not engaged context yet because too often the needs of the context drive the vision rather than the strategies. Notice the difference.

Let's consider a vision articulated by one team living among an unreached people group in West Africa.

> Our team has asked the question, "What will it look like when God's kingdom happens in this community?" The vision God has given us is one where people are once again in a right relationship with God, with each other, their environment and with themselves. There is improvement and transformation happening in every aspect of life (farming, health, community relationships, agriculture, education, clean water, etc.).... It is a place where there is shalom, where

God is king and he gets the glory. It is a place where people want to stay and those who have left want to come back to. It is also drawing attention from surrounding villages and becomes a movement that is spreading to other communities.

Given the needs of the community where they serve, it would have made sense for this team to arrive in the country and begin *doing* activities to meet needs—start a health clinic, give microloans, build a school, open an orphanage and conduct workshops on sustainable farming, as well as the heart of the church planting activities, evangelism and discipleship. These would all be seemingly logical activities given the needs of the context, but perhaps not the best strategies.

Ultimately these types of programs will not lead to the God-given vision of the team and may even dangerously establish dependency, leading to the stripping away of dignity, because the team, with their extensive education and resources, could from their own resources accomplish the activities named above. Yet, if they do these programs *for* the villagers, what does that communicate *to* the villagers? What does it do to the image of God present in each one? As parents, does it say they cannot take care of their own children? As leaders, does it say they cannot, in partnership with their whole community, solve the problems they really care about? That they are not smart human beings gifted with creativity and vision?

Dr. Dark visited the West Africa team for several weeks. He knew of the relatively high mortality rate of infants in the villages, and after observing for a few days, he felt he had some ideas for why the rates were high and what the mothers could do about it. So Dr. Dark and John, one of the team leaders, gathered the mothers and their babies, and with John interpreting, the doctor explained the pathology of the possible causes of infant mortality and what they, as mothers, could do differently.

John watched how the information affected the mothers. As the doctor spoke, they increasingly looked down and eventually did not meet his eyes. John felt their discomfort and shame. Not noticing, the doctor continued with his talk, telling them everything they were doing wrong, and then asked if they had questions. The mothers were silent.

John felt that he must do something to restore the dignity of the mothers, so he asked, "Some of you have been mothers for a long time and have had many children" (the older mothers looked up). "What kinds of things do you do to help your babies thrive?" One brave older woman shared some of her ways of mothering, which sparked others to share, until all the mothers were talking, sharing and learning from each other. Interestingly, the mothers already had the resources to address the problem; they just didn't realize it. John shared that the energy and life that was present amongst them was palpable after they had captured and shared the answers that would help their babies live.

Because John had articulated a God-inspired future, he knew that simply providing services was not enough. He knew they had to find ways to build up the people to help themselves. Their vision determined their strategies and activities.

ENGAGING THE CONTEXT

We can learn from the context to discern strategy in many ways. Ministers in crosscultural contexts often research and write ethnographies. Startup businesses conduct demographic and market surveys. Because of its applicability in most contexts, I offer the process of a SWOT analysis.

SWOT analyses are straightforward, interactive data-gathering processes, which encourage the possibility of everyone's participation. We look at our team or department or organization by considering four categories:

Strengths
Weaknesses
Opportunities
Threats

The first two letters in the SWOT acronym refer to characteristics within the organization and the other two consider factors outside.

SWOT analyses can be conducted on teams, in small groups or throughout the whole organization. Data gathering is similar for each. Facilitators encourage groups to brainstorm lists of the strengths and weaknesses of the organization. They then help the groups isolate commonalities and key emerging themes. An initial listing of categories is presented to the whole group or organization to ensure all pertinent information has been captured. Adjustments are made as necessary and then the facilitator, via discussion and/or voting, helps the group choose the most important (most critical for the mission and vision) four or five strengths and weaknesses.

The data gathering for opportunities and threats is more technical and requires much broader knowledge and information. I find that an initial defining of categories sparks people's thinking and encourages information gathering. Groups can brainstorm trends in their context as potential opportunities and threats. It can help to ask,

- What political, educational, demographic, societal, technological and religious trends do we notice in our context? (Consider these locally, regionally and globally.)
- What assets can you identify in your context? These are community resources, which could be thriving businesses, gatherings, leaders, special places where people meet, institutions, etc.

After an initial list of the trends, categorize these and ask,

- Are these trends opportunities and/or threats for our mission and vision?

These categories should be noted down, fed back to the whole group, adjusted and then re-presented. As in the strengths and weaknesses process, the most important (to the vision and mission) categories of opportunities and threats should be identified. After the SWOT data has been collected and prioritized, strategy development may commence.

DISCERNING STRATEGIES

Strategies are *how* the vision is accomplished. They are the *means* that move an organization toward the vision. Keeping the target—the articulated vision—at the forefront, place the lists of the strengths and opportunities side by side. The most fruitful strategies come from connecting strengths and opportunities. Notice if the strengths and opportunities relate to or correlate with each other. Keep in mind weaknesses and threats (and discern if some of the threats are actually opportunities), but because resources need to be directed with wise and effective stewardship, do not build strategies to address weaknesses or threats.

Because of the invasion of Jerusalem and the destruction of the temple in AD 70 by the Roman armies, the Jewish people were exiled and dispersed throughout the Roman Empire. On the surface, this was seemingly a threat to Judaism and especially the new, fledgling Jesus movement. However, Paul and his team, led by the Holy Spirit, developed a strategy by connecting strengths and opportunities. From the time they were first sent from Antioch, recorded in Acts 13, Paul and Barnabas traveled to cities in the Empire to proclaim the good news of Jesus Christ. Strategically, in each city the team would first visit the synagogue and preach (their strengths as mostly Jewish believers). If and when opposition became too great, they moved outside the synagogue and preached and taught in homes and the marketplace to any who gathered, including those who followed from the synagogue and the Gentiles. Eventually Paul and the team appointed elders to shepherd the new churches, and as directed by the Holy Spirit or when they were chased out of the city by the authorities, they moved on to the next cities (see Acts 13:13-52 and Acts 14:1-25).

Paul's strengths included a bicultural, cosmopolitan upbringing, multilingualism, and a Pharisaical education, all of which perfectly matched the opportunity contexts of exiled Jews in Greek/Roman cities. The strengths of his teams were often similar in that some were biracial (Timothy), multilingual, multicultural and so on.

Paul, again directed by the Spirit, carefully chose key cities that were influential for the surrounding contexts. This enabled the church to spread and grow in those regions and beyond because of connections to trade and travel.

Obviously resources will factor into the process of determining which opportunities to take advantage of, but faith-filled strategies can lead to faith-filled pursuit of resources.

Jim Collins offers a similar approach for discerning strategy called the Hedgehog Concept, so named from the Greek parable that extols the hedgehog for knowing one big thing.[1]

The Hedgehog, found at the intersection of the answer to these three questions, leads to effective strategic methods:

- What can we be the best in the world at?
- What drives your resource engine?[2]
- What are you deeply passionate about?

Before moving to goals and daily activities, however, I illustrate how strategies can be expressed as results.

OUTPUTS VS. OUTCOMES

Consider the difference in these two descriptions shared by Damon to his board.

Description 1. Last year we had 100 volunteers working in three different ministries: tutoring elementary students, mentoring high school students and serving meals to homeless people. As a result, 60 children received 9,000 hours of tutoring, 40 high school students connected for 72 hours with their mentors, and 2,400 meals were served to homeless people.

Description 2. Last year we partnered with 100 volunteers. They felt confident in their various ministries because of our extensive training program, and as a result, they were inspired by the many ways God brought forth fruit through them. The reading and math scores of 60 children increased by 20 percent. 100 percent of the mentored high school students stayed in school, implemented plans to finish high school, and set goals for vocational training or university after their graduation. We redirected income from the homeless meals to another ministry that through a six-month placement and vocational training facilitates homeless families off the streets permanently.

These paragraphs illustrate the difference between measuring outputs and outcomes. Ultimately, because vision is expressed as an outcome, a picture of a result in the future, characterizing and measuring strategies as outcomes helps the organization stay on target toward the vision. Outputs (the first description) alternatively quantifies numbers of people who attend events or programs, items produced as a result of inputs, time spent in activities, and so on—not the results or outcomes of the events, inputs or activities. Creating outcome statements for specific strategies acts as a bridge between vision and goals, to which we now turn.

GOAL SETTING AND PLANNING

After considering the context, discerning possible strategies and creating outcome targets, it is time to fully implement mission and vision on the ground by setting goals and deciding who is doing what. Writing goals translates big-picture vision into time and space. Planning puts it all into motion.

Churches and Christian organizations often shy away from creating goals for two reasons: (1) the practice feels unspiritual, too technical, and seemingly, Jesus did not write goals; (2) people fear disappointment. What if the organization or team does not attain its goals? How will people feel? What will happen to morale?

These perspectives have credence. Sometimes setting goals can be manipulative and gimmicky. And it is true, not reaching one's goals can be disappointing. However, writing faith-filled goals is another step in the process of translating faith-filled vision and hoped-for outcomes into daily reality, and goals provide a means for ongoing accountability; therefore, it is an important process.

In chapter six and table 6.1 I mention the acronym SMARTER, which provides a useful framework for writing goals. Goals, flowing from mission, vision, strategies and outcomes, and shaped by values, should be Specific, Measurable, Achievable, Relevant, Time oriented, Evaluated and Reviewed. Writing SMARTER goals enables people to determine if they are on target since they readily signal something measurable.

Let's say my church has a vision for reproducing contextual (neighborhoods, various marketplace vocations) mission outposts (simple churches) that proclaim and live the kingdom of God. It will need a strategy for reproducing and developing leaders. Stated as an outcome, "We mobilized and equipped competent leaders who announced the kingdom of God and pastored groups of people in their contexts."

A SMARTER goal directed toward this strategy could be written as, "By December 31, we will mobilize and train ten new leaders for five new missional outposts. We will evaluate progress toward this goal at our weekly staff meetings and review the goal on December 31." Note that the writing of the SMARTER goal introduces the need for more strategic thinking, as there will be multiple ways my church could accomplish this goal. For example, we could target specific industries (e.g., film and music) where our members work, or we could target specific groups of people such as families with young children or neighborhoods or those interested in some type of sociopolitical issue. Then, there are multiple ways to invite (announcement in church services, personal invitations, appointments with the elders, etc.) and train (retreats, meeting every week, sharing faith stories, practice preaching, etc.) these new pastors for their respective mission outposts.

Once particular strategies directed to the SMARTER goals are chosen, planning may commence. The size or comprehensiveness of the goal will determine what type of planning is needed.

Some SMARTER goals can be directly translated into *who* will do *what* by *when* and with what *resources*. Others are more complex and therefore need greater depth of planning that includes a comprehensive timeline, promotion, preparation and plans.

Returning to the previous example regarding the initiative to develop leaders for mission outposts, let's say that it is now September 1 and recruitment of the leaders has taken place. (Remember, the goal is ten new, fully trained leaders for five new mission outposts by December 31.) The church leaders decided that two Friday night and all-day Saturday sessions would best serve these busy, marketplace leaders. One session is planned for mid-October and the other for mid-November. Regarding the timeline, facilitators must decide what needs to happen immediately as well as one month before, one week before, and the day before the training events. This planning could include pre-session, in-between session, and post-session assignments, finding a venue for the training and preparing the training materials. In case some of the plans do not work, contingency scenarios must be considered to still achieve the goal.

We have considered the specifics of translating vision and mission into the daily realities of context, outcomes, strategies, goals and plans. We should also be able to measure how our goals and plans lead to the vision and mission—a constant feedback loop.

15

ONE ORGANIZATION'S STORY

Prison Fellowship was founded in the United States by Charles Colson after he was imprisoned following the Watergate scandal. Prison Fellowship International (PFI) was then formed in 1979 and eventually incorporated in over 125 countries, each with their own boards and autonomous organization. The international umbrella, PFI, however, did not grow at the same pace, and in fact, due to lack of funding, began shrinking in 2004.

The funding scheme for PFI was based on an association model—countries become members of PFI through a clearly defined process, ensuring shared vision and values. They pay membership dues, "charter fees," yearly based on the national ministry's donations. This schema worked fine when developed nations were the primary members of the organization. However, the vast majority of new members in more recent years came from the lowest-income countries in the world.

An increase in countries and service needs without an increase in revenue decreased PFI's spending ability by 30 percent. More countries were in need of service with less means to serve. Moreover, the recession beginning in 2008 negatively impacted giving in the high-income nations such as the USA, UK, Germany and Australia. PFI revenue took another hit. A steady practice of cost cutting and layoffs eventually meant that PFI endeavored to serve over 125 national ministries with 30 percent fewer staff, and the newly established organizations in already difficult circumstances languished, leaving 40 percent unsustainable. Something had to change.

A BOLD DECISION AND BRUTAL FACTS

In 2012, PFI leaders understood a membership-fee funding model could not remain the major revenue source. They boldly decided that PFI should not depend on the membership fees, especially from the US (because of the large budget of Prison Fellowship Ministries, the US provided 90 percent of the total budget of PFI), but they would create a new revenue model and a fundraising initiative. Not an easy venture. Imagine, a thirty-four-year-old not-for-profit organization that had never raised support and had no donors!

As the board and leaders of PFI grappled with the implications of their leap of faith, they wondered, would their mission and vision be compelling to donors?[1] Were they on target for their vision? Were they reaching the outcomes that would lead to their vision? Was there a way to be more effective and impactful? Was their DNA intact?

The team initiated a research project to ascertain the answer to these and other questions. Researchers interviewed representatives from PFI's member nations, endeavoring to learn the scope and impact of their ministry as it relates to the vision. What programs are effective? Is there a meaningful Christian presence in every prison of their country? Is the gospel message transforming prisoners, their families and those impacted by crime?

The researchers discovered that PFI engages 31 percent of the prisons in the countries of their affiliates. They also found that 84 percent of these ministries conduct some type of spiritual formation for prisoners using a variety methods—Alpha, Celebrate Recovery, Christianity Explored, evangelistic campaigns and unstructured Bible studies. They learned that 95 percent of PFI affiliates have ministry among children of prisoners, whether through Angel Tree or other activities such as camps, kid's clubs, tutoring, counseling, letter writing or videos to incarcerated parents and so forth. On average, fifty thousand volunteers partner with Prison Fellowship each year. The research findings also affirmed a key aspect of PFI's DNA: affiliates comprise all the major Christian traditions—Protestant, Catholic, Orthodox and Pentecostal/Charismatic.

BUILDING ON STRENGTHS

Could PFI intensely focus toward capacity development to increase the effectiveness of the national ministries? If they created effective, contextual programs focused toward children of prisoners and evangelization, could they increase the impact of their affiliates? Instead of over 125 affiliates could there be prison fellowships in every country of the world where there are prisons? Or could they increase the number of prisons they have a presence in from 31 percent to 100 percent in the countries they already serve? Or knowing the plight of children of prisoners—destitution, slavery, and the likelihood of becoming offenders—could they partner with national ministries to ensure children have the opportunity to break the cycle of crime? God captured the leaders' imaginations and began to breathe life and faith into possible strategies.

Further research led to the discovery that in most countries, children of prisoners are the most vulnerable of the vulnerable. Children with incarcerated parents are seven times more likely than other children to be imprisoned. In some countries, children are even in prison with their parent. In some, they starve or live on the streets because the breadwinner is incarcerated. In some, children of prisoners are sold into slavery by relatives or even their own parent because there isn't enough food to feed the whole family. PFI leaders know that if the cycle of crime and incarceration can be broken in a child's life, the whole society is affected.

STRENGTHS + OPPORTUNITIES = STRATEGIES

Two contextual opportunities emerged as well. First, *Christianity Today* published a study from economist Bruce Wydick addressing the impact of child sponsorship.[2] The study, conducted primarily in 2010, researched seven countries where Compassion International connects impoverished children with sponsors. The findings of the study purport that child sponsorship is one of the most influential ways to end poverty. The researchers found that "sponsorship makes children 27 to 40 percent more likely to complete secondary school, and 50 to 80 percent more likely to complete a university education."

Inspired by this study, PFI's researchers contacted Compassion and acquired more information about the research from their perspective. Compassion eagerly offered counsel and in these conversations, PFI researchers learned that Compassion did not have programs or other interventions that addressed the unique problems of children of prisoners. This sparked an idea: could PFI create a child sponsorship program for children of prisoners? PFI pursued the idea with Compassion for advice and next steps. Gaining confirmation from advisors and the board, they engaged a consulting company that helped them design a children of prisoners sponsorship program.

The second opportunity was uncovered when the CEO made a courtesy visit to the CEO of Christianity Explored (CE) in London.[3] He discovered that CE adapted their popular evangelism program for use in prisons, and it was effective already in fifty prisons in the UK. As they discussed, the CEOs realized an immense opportunity for partnership. PFI was creating an evangelization program that would increase the effectiveness of their affiliates. CE wanted to have access and distribute CE in prisons around the world. Eventually, PFI and CE signed an agreement and formalized their partnership to develop an evangelization program contextually appropriate for prisoners around the world.

These two contextual opportunities led to the creation and development of two strategic programs, the Children of Prisoners Partnership (CPP) and The Prisoner's Journey (TPJ). National ministries that have capacity have the opportunity to partner with PFI to implement these programs. While the programs have foundational requirements (for example, CPP must ensure children's safety, health, education and spiritual resilience), PFI and country leaders design and implement the program according to what's appropriate for their context and already-existing ministry. The programs provided impetus for donors, yet an overall funding strategy was still needed, since PFI could not rely on membership fees as their sole source of funding.

PEOPLE

Excitement and momentum built as these opportunities led to new realities. Yet the leaders realized that creating the two programs and fundraising would require certain skills and focused organizational energy. They were moving from being an association model, where PFI provided services if and when the affiliates wanted, to a leadership model, where PFI would lead the organization toward outcomes and impact. Everyone's time and talents would need redirection. Some staff left or were laid off due to issues of fit. Some of these were painful departures. New employees were hired who had the skills and expertise needed for the future.

Meanwhile, organizational leaders stayed laser focused on the change, which was a challenge, especially when word got out about the programs. Affiliates wondered if PFI was losing its way or drifting from the mission and vision.

To circumvent opposition and, more importantly, to demonstrate PFI's commitment to their DNA while at the same time introducing PFI 2.0, organizational leaders designed regional leadership summits for every continent of the world. Representatives from PFI's 127 member nations gathered to interact with leaders and hear the future direction of PFI, and especially learn about the programs. The theme of the conferences, Preserve the Past, Pursue the Future, provided the framework by which organizational leaders could demonstrate their commitment to PFI's DNA, while striving toward a bright future.

OPERATIONS

Not unexpectedly, the new direction necessitated changes in other aspects of the organization as well, such as their operations. In fact, aspects of PFI needed a complete overhaul.

Prior to 2014, PFI had few donors. Organizational leaders devised plans to share the vision of PFI and promote the ministry, especially the new programs. They contracted with a fundraising agency, which implemented direct mailing initiatives from which donors could be nurtured. The agency also produced direct response TV slots, highlighting the Children of Prisoners initiative. The leaders presented the PFI initiatives to major donors and submitted proposals to appropriate foundations. The overall funding plan included targets for five years, which decreased PFI's reliance on charter fees year by year.

Program managers created systems and policies for qualifying national ministries for the new programs. They developed training in order to equip people to effectively run the program partnerships, which included not only the essence of effective programs but sound financial management as well. New systems were also needed for monitoring and evaluation. New technology in finance and donor management enabled PFI to more efficiently expedite gifts and track donor care and involvement.

Technology also aided Children of Prisoners sponsorship through the website, allowing donors to prayerfully select the children they would sponsor. And speaking of websites, PFI created two new ones—one for external focus and marketing and a second for the national affiliates that provided a directory, resources and training.

PFI's comprehensive organizational change propelled the organization into growth and impact. At the time of this writing, the transition is nearing its midpoint, and there are a number of indications that it is working. Donors are responding. The Children of Prisoners pilot countries have done well, and now the program is being fully rolled out. The initial results of The Prisoner's Journey have exceeded expectations. PFI leaders continue to pray that the ministry has moved from a languishing to a flourishing organization.

16

FLOURISHING ORGANIZATIONS

We have journeyed through the many and complex components of flourishing organizations. The case study in chapter fifteen demonstrates the comprehensive approach required for moving a languishing organization to a flourishing organization, including focused and sometimes painful work. It's time now to encapsulate the previous chapters into a comprehensive description of the flourishing organization.

As stated before, organizations are people. A flourishing organization, whether a church, NGO, business, mission agency, or other not-for-profit company, is a community of people called together for a purpose. Flourishing Christian organizations—churches and companies—exist for the greater purposes of God's kingdom. They pronounce and live in God's freedom-producing, life-giving, holistic reign. Living in God's reign, people in these organizations experience the wildness, adventure, fruitfulness and abundant life of God's kingdom and invite others to do so as well.

A called community that participates in God's mission is unique. How each community participates in the kingdom will be different. Ultimately, Christian organizations should be flourishing, thriving organizations because that reflects their Creator's image.

We started *Made to Flourish* by defining flourishing organizations as
- vibrant, reproducing, kingdom-of-God communities
- called together to live in God's reign and join God's mission to proclaim and live in his kingdom and to, by God's enabling grace,
- pursue their unique, God-given purpose and
- produce God's vision of the future
- while creating an environment where individuals thrive.

Flourishing organizations are fun, satisfying, safe environments where individuals are restored and embrace transformation into the image of Christ. They live the authentic Jesus life—attractive, joyful and contagious.

While each organization distinctively lives out its purpose and, hopefully, increasingly lives God's vision of the future, there are general components of flourishing organizations. Let me review these elements.
- The life force of a flourishing organization—its vision, mission, values and faith assumptions—its DNA—is centered in
- a called, committed community shaped by the organization's faith assumptions and values

- that accomplishes its vision and mission in the reality of each context, which requires constant research and analysis, and leads to
- effective strategies and
- subsequent operations, appropriate for the organization's values and which form the vision/mission and that support the strategies to produce
- growth and sustainability.

Figure 16.1 synthesizes all this into one, holistic picture. Let me give a picture of what each component would look like, fully flourishing.[1]

COMPONENTS OF A FLOURISHING ORGANIZATION

DNA—life force of an organization. An organization's life force is its vision, mission, faith assumptions and values. Every aspect of a flourishing organization flows from and connects with its DNA. All strategies emerge from and are evaluated by the vision and mission; they are shaped by the values and faith assumptions. All structures, procedures and systems exist to enable the accomplishment of mission and vision.

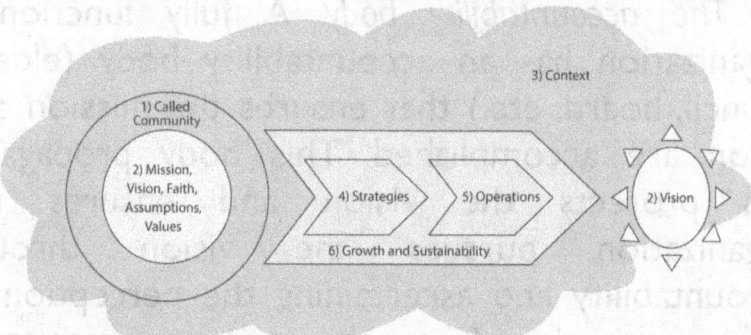

Figure 16.1. The components of a flourishing organization

People. The people who reproduce the DNA are a called, committed community. The vision, mission, faith assumptions and values permeate, motivate and constrain the people of flourishing organizations. Everyone associated with the ministry is on pilgrimage from minimal awareness to full participation in and replication of the DNA, including the following.

Leaders. Organizations thrive with a dedicated team of prayerful, Christ-shaped leaders who embody the DNA and may or may not be positional leaders in the organization.[2] These leaders adapt, innovate and create, so as to continually reproduce and pursue the vision. They are competent, character driven and fully dedicated. Others are attracted to the organization's vision and mission through these leaders, and they constantly multiply, develop and release other leaders into the organization or other kingdom work.

The accountability body. A fully functioning organization has an accountability body (elders, council, board, etc.) that ensures the mission and vision are accomplished. This body propagates and protects the vision and ensures the organization pursues the vision through accountability and ascertaining the perception of the organization from the wider constituency (external constituencies discern if the organization does the mission). If a board, it has representation from and linkage with critical constituencies. It creates an ideal board profile, which provides needed expertise according to the mission and context, and pursues board members who meet the profile. The accountability body exemplifies excellent governance through strong relationships with the organizational leader(s) (leadership team, executive director, CEO, president, etc.), its own development, term limits, written bylaws, governance policies and processes, and regular self-evaluation.

Partners. Flourishing organizations attract more and more people—staff, church members, volunteers and donors. They create a context-specific process of development that invites and educates people along a continuum from simple awareness of the organization's activities to active involvement in the ministry. In this committed community, whether full-time staff, members or marketplace ministers, there is a sense of belonging, mutuality and kingdom-oriented mission.

Networks. Knowing that any faith-filled, kingdom-of-God vision is beyond one community's efforts, flourishing organizations look for partnerships. A maturing organization has an ever-expanding, intentional network of individuals and organizations connected to and concerned about the ministry.

Context and research. Vision must connect with four realities:

The reality of the wider context, including the global context. Ongoing research enables leaders to be aware of educational, political, religious, social and technological trends that may offer opportunities or impact the organization in some manner.

The reality of the target context. The vision connects with a deep understanding of the assets, strengths, needs, demographics, trends and life situations of those the organization seeks to serve.

The reality of the organization's uniqueness, strengths and weaknesses. An organization needs to be aware of its particular assets, resources and experiences as well as its limitations.

The reality of like-minded organizations. This interconnectedness leads to interdependence, cross-pollination, awareness of best practices, and support of and participation in each other's mission. It allows an organization to more fully accomplish its vision and mission than it could on its own.

Strategies. Strategies, the means for doing the mission, are compelled by and evaluated according to the vision, mission, faith assumptions and values. Strategies connect with the assets and the real needs of the context, intersecting these through life-giving innovation. Strategies often become reality through programs or other activities. Nonetheless, strategies and programs should never be set in stone. They can and must change for opportunities, changing circumstances and innovation so that the vision is accomplished.

Ultimately, strategies must be described in outcomes, the actual resulting change that the strategy brings, and goals (remember, SMARTER goals). Then, planning, further strategizing and evaluating enable the goals to be fulfilled.

Operations. The vision is supported by efficient, scalable communication, finance, human resource and management systems. While these systems, like strategies, should never become more important than the vision, mission, faith assumptions and values, they are supportive for the overall success of the organization.

Communication. Tell the stories, tell the stories, tell the stories! Flourishing organizations communicate the stories of God's interventions. If the organization is multinational, flourishing organizations strive for interdependence in the global family. They tell stories that capture the

DNA globally as well as locally. One country's stories are the whole movement's stories.

Flourishing organizations also strive for constant, transparent and cascading communication from the leadership team to everyone in the organization. They deal with conflict immediately (in culturally appropriate ways), as unresolved conflict becomes cancer in organizations, eroding trust and eventually morale.

Flourishing organizations use technology (websites, social media, etc.) to leverage wider communication. And they do this following strict kingdom ethics of respect, protecting each person's dignity and humanity.

Finance. Flourishing organizations need efficient means for reviewing, evaluating (constrained by the DNA), planning and budgeting. They have high standards for internal controls, and systems are in place to prevent the misuse of funds. Accounting should be established according to international accounting standards with thorough accountability and audits. Financial reports, receipting, celebrating and thank-yous must be timely and regular.

Human resources. Employees and volunteer partners thrive when they connect meaningfully with the ministry, including being given roles they both understand and fit. This process includes applications, job descriptions, roles and responsibilities, orientation, training, feedback, encouragement and constant development. Focus must be given to create a developmental environment where all involved experience care, spiritual growth, mentoring, celebration and so on.

All legal HR standards and requirements of the country must be known and met. Flourishing organizations have respectful and fair management and supervision processes. They have an HR policy that can accommodate change and transition in strategy, especially when staff numbers are increased or reduced, or other dynamics change (e.g., moving from staff to volunteers or vice versa).

Management. A reproducible and contextualized system for mobilizing funding and people for programs, events and projects is necessary in a flourishing organization. Projects and events become reproducible with these key elements: prayer, stated outcomes (statement of the actual resulting change), goals (specific, measurable, achievable, relevant, time oriented, evaluated and reviewed), action plans (who does what by when and with what resources), evaluation and documentation. Production templates or documenting in some way enables reproducibility in following years or other contexts.

Technology. For all the above, appropriate technology is utilized. Alongside strong interpersonal relationships, leaders, or others in the organization, must stay abreast of timesaving, efficient, redundancy-reducing, promotional innovations, for example, streamlined donor research, accounting and personnel systems, or use of the Cloud.

Growth and sustainability. Flourishing assumes newness, growth, creativity and innovation. Flourishing organizations innovate for constant growth and to address the target of their vision. Pronounced entrepreneurialism signals sustainability and life. A culture of entrepreneurialism is fostered and protected. New ideas, strategies, programs and experiments are pursued until the vision is accomplished—or until Jesus Christ returns. The organization attracts and nurtures entrepreneurs. It has rhythms and structures for entrepreneurial activities.

Flourishing organizations grow and reproduce. The vision is so compelling that it attracts more and more people. The people involved in the organization experience growth and transformation in their life with Christ. They constantly learn, grow and develop. They become increasingly more effective kingdom-of-God participants and partners as a result of their experience in the organization. They reproduce the excellent training they receive in churches and the marketplace. Partnerships with other like-minded ministries offer holistic, comprehensive scalability until the vision is reached.

Flourishing organizations are characterized by psychological and financial ownership. All those associated with the ministry sense their belonging, and participation is integral. Developed organizations that are not for profit acquire funding from diverse sources—government and agencies (if appropriate and it does not compromise the vision and values), grants, donors, gifts-in-kind, programs, products and services. The executive leaders spend 15 to 25 percent of their time cultivating diverse resources. They implement funding plans that include strategies for large numbers of small donations, major donations, grants, etc. The flourishing organization cares for their donors with timely thank-yous and receipts and ultimately through friendship and service.

MADE TO FLOURISH

Because of the contexts and the callings, the components will look different in each organization.[3] Therefore, organizational leaders must first collaboratively research and collect data and come to an agreement on what their organization would look like if it were flourishing. What do they imagine and hope will be the future of their organization? If the organization does what God has called it to do and achieves the outcomes for which it exists, what will that look like? What will people see, feel and experience? What difference will it make in society and how is the difference described? Answering these questions in a participatory process will eventually lead to an individual, contextual profile of a flourishing organization—the destination toward which people in the organization can then journey.

I've pictured the ideal flourishing organization in this chapter. As this book has described, however, becoming flourishing is a developmental process. When we are aware of the characteristics of flourishing in the ECO model, these can act as signposts for us as we seek to help our team, our department or our organization flourish.

ACKNOWLEDGMENTS

Over the years, numerous mentors and partners contributed to my spiritual, leadership and organizational formation. I especially highlight Joel Olson, Geri Rodman, Bobby Clinton, Dan and Lindie Bacon, David Dougherty, Timothy Khoo and Frank Lofaro, as well as those who have journeyed with me in the crucible of leadership—my communities in Pasadena and Singapore. Hundreds of students contributed their organizations' stories, which shaped the outcome of *Made to Flourish*. Andy Le Peau, my editor, helped capture my voice and tone down my sometimes too intuitive or technical language.

Thank you to all.

Appendix I

TECHNICAL ASPECTS OF FLOURISHING

The concept of flourishing has only recently been applied to organizational settings, and mostly as it relates to mental health and its absence (mental illness) in the work context.[1] According to positive psychology researcher Corey Keyes, only 20 percent of Americans flourish, while up to one third actually languish.[2] One definition of flourishing is "to live within an optimal range of human functioning, one that connotes goodness, generativity, growth, and resilience," while "languishing" refers to "people who describe their lives as 'hollow' or 'empty.'"[3] It is doubtful that the discipline of positive psychology founds itself on Genesis 1, but one does get the sense that "flourishing" is what God intends:

> Then God said, "Let the earth put forth vegetation: plants yielding seed, and fruit trees of every kind on earth that bear fruit with the seed in it." And it was so.... And God said, "Let the waters bring forth swarms of living creatures, and let birds fly above the earth across the dome of the sky." ... God blessed them, saying, "Be

fruitful and multiply and fill the waters in the seas, and let birds multiply on the earth." ... And God said, "Let the earth bring forth living creatures of every kind: cattle and creeping things and wild animals of the earth of every kind." And it was so.... Then God said, "Let us make humankind in our image, according to our likeness; and let them have dominion over the fish of the sea, and over the birds of the air, and over the cattle, and over all the wild animals of the earth, and over every creeping thing that creeps upon the earth." ... God blessed them, and God said to them, "Be fruitful and multiply, and fill the earth and subdue it; and have dominion over the fish of the sea and over the birds of the air and over every living thing that moves upon the earth." (Gen 1:11, 20, 22, 24, 26, 28)

Flourishing is also what Jesus envisions when quoting the prophet Isaiah in Luke 4.

The Spirit of the Lord is upon me,
because he has anointed me
to bring good news to the poor.
He has sent me to proclaim release to the captives
and recovery of sight to the blind,
to let the oppressed go free,
to proclaim the year of the Lord's favor.
(Lk 4:18-19, ref. Is 61:1-2)

And I believe flourishing is our ultimate hope in the picture of the future found in Revelation.

> Then I saw a new heaven and a new earth; for the first heaven and the first earth had passed away, and the sea was no more. And I saw the holy city, the new Jerusalem, coming down out of heaven from God, prepared as a bride adorned for her husband. And I heard a loud voice from the throne saying,
> "See, the home of God is among mortals.
> He will dwell with them;
> they will be his peoples,
> and God himself will be with them;
> he will wipe every tear from their eyes.
> Death will be no more;
> mourning and crying and pain will be no more,
> for the first things have passed away." (Rev 21:1-4)

> Then the angel showed me the river of the water of life, bright as crystal, flowing from the throne of God and of the Lamb through the middle of the street of the city. On either side of the river is the tree of life with its twelve kinds of fruit, producing its fruit each month; and the leaves of the tree are for the healing of the nations. (Rev 22:1-2)

As is so often the case, contemporary research unearths, highlights and connects with biblical themes and values. The concept of flourishing underscores this tendency.

When humans flourish, according to Keyes, they experience emotional, psychological and social well-being.[4] In general, they are "full of life," "peaceful," "cheerful" and "satisfied."[5] They accept themselves and know of their strengths and weaknesses. They engage challenges, enjoy learning and embrace an overall sense of purpose. Each day is useful and hopeful. Flourishing people have strong relationships and connectedness to community, contributing as well as receiving. They are curious about differences and suspend judgment for optimized learning.

One notes the emphasis on positive emotions, and they are also key aspects of flourishing, especially related to creative productivity. Barbara Fredrickson's research proposes that

> negative emotions function to narrow a person's momentary thought-action repertoire. They do so by calling to mind and body the time-tested, ancestrally adaptive actions represented by specific action tendencies.... Positive emotions prompt individuals to discard time-tested or automatic (everyday) behavioral scripts and to pursue novel, creative, and often unscripted paths of thought and action.[6]

She labels this phenomenon the "broaden-and-build theory," and I connect it to the theology of God's image in us. Humans, created in God's image,[7] are meant to flourish, and in that flourishing they learn and become co-creators with God. In flourishing environments, they pursue meaning and purpose. They innovate and adapt to adjust in new situations or when faced with challenges. Therefore, I propose that kingdom-of-God-oriented organizations,[8] whether churches, NGOs, mission agencies, other nonprofits or businesses, ultimately should be entities that flourish. In other words, in a flourishing organization, everything and everyone is thriving.[9]

Appendix 2

FLOURISHING DEVELOPMENTAL ASSESSMENT TOOL

The following sections provide continuums that describe movement toward flourishing for each of the six components of flourishing organizations. Used in conjunction with the descriptive portrayal of flourishing organizations earlier in chapter sixteen, the assessment provides signposts for different phases in an organization's growth toward flourishing. The assessment offers reasonable developmental expectations of what an organization will experience and need to anticipate as it grows.

Considering your organization, read through the descriptors from left to right for each category in each component. Match your organization's characteristics to the descriptors. Note: the descriptions in the tables are cumulative and build from left to right.

COMPONENT 1: DNA—VISION, MISSION, VALUES, FAITH ASSUMPTIONS

To what extent is the organization aligned with its vision, mission, values and faith assumptions?

Capacity Element	Not Active	Phase One	Phase Two	Phase Three	Phase Four	Capacity Rating
Vision		Vision rarely referenced.	Vision understood, often stated, and guides strategies.	Vision guides activities, connects with results and outcomes, and is used for evaluation and development.	Vision provides a clear picture of future. The vision is regularly referenced and is at the core of operations, able to be articulated and lived by the majority of people associated with the ministry.	
Mission		Mission rarely referenced.	Organization understands its purpose and the mission is often referenced.	Mission understood, often stated, and guides strategies leading to effective programs, activities, initiatives, etc.	Mission compels and is at the core of operations, able to be articulated and lived by the majority of people associated with the ministry.	
Values		Values rarely referenced and not explicit.	Values articulated but not widely known.	Values guide strategy development, leading to unique, effective activities toward the vision.	Values intentionally determine direction when there's competing alternatives and during crises. Full integrity between espoused and demonstrated values.	
Faith Assumptions		Biblical/theological reasoning rarely referenced and not explicit.	Biblical/theological foundations articulated as part of the story of the organization.	Biblical/theological foundations guide strategy development, leading to unique, effective activities toward the vision.	Biblical/theological foundations intentionally determine direction when there's competing alternatives and during crises. Full integrity between espoused and demonstrated faith assumptions.	

COMPONENT 2: A CALLED COMMUNITY COMMITTED TO VISION, MISSION, VALUES AND FAITH ASSUMPTIONS

To what extent do people demonstrate Christlike character? To what extent are people involved in the organization?

Capacity Element	Not Active	Phase One	Phase Two	Phase Three	Phase Four	Capacity Rating
Leaders' Spirituality		Prayerful, Christ-transformed, biblically informed.	Competent, experienced, character-driven, balanced life.	Tested and community-affirmed sense of call to the ministry.	Fully committed to the vocation.	
Leaders' Vision & Mission		Sometimes refer to the vision, mission.	Structures daily activities and goals according to the vision, mission.	Clearly articulates and attracts others to the vision, mission.	Reproduces and develops other leaders and partners committed to the vision, mission.	
Contextual Leaders		Understands needs of local context.	Stays abreast of contextual trends.	Studies disciplines that may increase effectiveness of the organization.	Draws from a cross-section of disciplines, studies larger social contexts and incorporates other entities' experiences.	
Leaders' Development		Ministry orientation provided for key leadership.	Training and development plan designed and implemented.	Strategy for leadership development in place, including recruitment, mentoring and continuing education.	Long-term leadership development strategy for sustainability and succession fully implemented.	
Board Members		Primarily leader's friends and contacts committed to vision, mission and values.	Increasing members from diverse backgrounds, committed to, active and participating in vision, mission and values.	Board members attract other members who contribute diverse expertise.	Ideal board profile with representation from and linkage with critical constituencies relevant to the strategies and needs of the organization.	

Capacity Element	Not Active	Phase One	Phase Two	Phase Three	Phase Four	Capacity Rating
Board Governance		Provides accountability for the primary leader of the organization. Written bylaws, constitution.	Ensures the DNA of the organization by evaluating connection of activities to the vision, mission and values.	Full board manual that includes governance policies and process, board development and self-evaluation.	Board evaluates the organization through their linkages to external constituencies and their perceptions of the organization.	
Board—Executive Relationship		Board and executive have a shared burden for ministry responsibilities.	Board and executive functions distinguished.	Frequent bilateral communication, including functioning reporting structures. Regular evaluation of primary organization's leader (e.g., CEO, president).	Collaborative and cooperative partnership in roles, responsibilities and authority.	
Volunteers/ Partners		Relational connections of organization's leader participate in ministry.	Increasing numbers of people give time and money to programs, events and activities of the organization.	Volunteers/partners respond to the organization's mission and become fully involved as well as attract other volunteers/partners.	Regular, thriving volunteers/partners involved in programs, including planning, decision making, organizing, leading and evaluating.	
Volunteers/ Partners Mobilization		Volunteers enrolled sporadically and drawn from a few contacts of leadership.	Volunteer recruitment and placement plan developed to meet existing ministry needs.	Well-trained and equipped volunteers in specialized areas mobilized to capitalize on ministry opportunities.	Formalized, extensive volunteer base and volunteer management plan effected, thus ensuring sustainable growth.	

COMPONENT 3: CONTEXT AND RESEARCH

To what extent does the organization understand its context?

Capacity Element	Not Active	Phase One	Phase Two	Phase Three	Phase Four	Capacity Rating
Target Context		Generalized knowledge of target focus of the mission.	Research leading to understanding of target focus.	Ongoing research and connection to target focus leads to adjustment in strategies and activities.	Ongoing research and comprehensive understanding leads to breakthrough, experimental strategies and activities.	
Wider Context		Little attention to context trends and influences.	Aware of political and governmental trends.	Aware of political, economic, educational, demographic, social, technological and religious trends.	Continuous research and awareness of political, economic, educational, demographic, social, technological and religious trends leads to breakthrough, experimental strategies and activities.	
If the organization is a national or global movement		General awareness of organization's history and structures.	Attend regional and international training and gatherings. Cross-pollination strengthens the organization.	Actively seek learning of best practices and creativity in other contexts.	Strong interdependence with the global movement. Stronger organizations coach, share resources and help other regional/global organizations develop.	

COMPONENT 4: STRATEGIES TOWARD OUTCOMES

To what extent are the organization's strategies based on the context and lead to outcomes flowing from the vision and mission?

Capacity Element	Not Active	Phase One	Phase Two	Phase Three	Phase Four	Capacity Rating
Strategies		Ad hoc activities based on other ministries.	Strategies connected to the context and outcomes based.	Deep understanding of context, experimentation with many different approaches, activities and programs.	Strategies defined and documented, including steps/pathways. Constant evaluation of strategies and experimentation leads to breakthrough, reproducible strategies that lead to the vision.	
Scope/Scale		Few programs/activities directed toward target focus.	Increasing programs/activities directed toward target focus.	Reproducing programs/activities in other contexts leads to growth of organization.	Comprehensive portfolio of effective programs/activities leads to saturation of target focus.	
Program Design & Development		Programs developed in ad hoc manner.	Design and development of programs as per identified needs.	Creative innovations, pilot testing and evaluation as a basis for decisions on program viability.	Accurate identification and implementation of relevant and effective programs to identified constituencies, with documented designs/plan.	
Program Monitoring and Evaluation (M & E) Toward Impact		No or very little M & E, ad hoc documentation.	Basic M & E system covering outputs and some documentation of results.	M & E system covering outputs, outcomes and impact.	Accurate and comprehensive M & E system covering outputs, outcomes and impact toward the vision.	

COMPONENT 5: OPERATIONS

To what extent are the organization's operations efficient, ethical and supportive of the mission and vision?

Capacity Element	Not Active	Phase One	Phase Two	Phase Three	Phase Four	Capacity Rating
Communication (internal)		Two-way communication among various components of ministry structure.	Regular and frequent meetings and written communiqués among board, staff and volunteers.	Strong interdependence and story sharing. Appropriate conflict resolution.	Integrated flow of formal and informal communication through comprehensive ministry network.	
Communication (external)		Regular and informational communication with donors—receipts and thank-you letters.	Use of website and other media to promote, explain and fund the ministry. Criteria for ethical use of media in place.	Specialized meetings and targeted communication with key constituencies. Use marketing principles for effective connection with context.	Advanced use of technology and social media.	
Finance		Bookkeeping maintained as per legal requirements. Yearly budgets are funded and fully implemented.	Financial records maintained, and basic policies and procedures established for resource utilization and protection from misuse of funds. Organization has secure systems for monitoring and managing expenditures.	Review and analysis lead to budget creation for effective resource utilization. Organization has annual, independent audits and implementation of recommendations from the audits.	Operational and strategic short- and long-range plans and budgets funded and fully implemented. Fund development plans in place.	

Capacity Element	Not Active	Phase One	Phase Two	Phase Three	Phase Four	Capacity Rating
Human Resources		Ad hoc staff and/or volunteer utilization.	Basic recruitment, placement and monitoring of staff and/or volunteers. Job descriptions for all staff and volunteers. Annual reviews, including development goals, for all staff and key volunteers.	Planned recruitment, selection, training, placement and supervision of staff and/or volunteers.	Comprehensive and integrated personnel management plan and strategy fully implemented. Use of website, social media for mobilization.	
Infrastructure		Dedicated office space, shared or rented.	Dedicated office space that is equipped.	Office space conducive to productive work and visibly demonstrates vision, mission and values.	Office space a vibrant hub of administrative and other activities.	
Management		Informal, unwritten guidelines and/or directions in place.	Short-term plans formulated to meet challenges and opportunities, with policies and procedures in place. Operational policies and procedures are in place.	Planning includes stated outcomes (specific and measurable), goals (specific, measurable, achievable, reality based, time oriented), action plans (who does what by when and with what resources).	Annual evaluation and documentation of operational and program activities.	
Technology		System for beneficiary and financial data. System for accounting and receipting.	Regular evaluation leading to greater efficiency for finance and personnel systems.	Learning and use of consultants leads to timesaving, efficient, redundancy-reducing, promotional innovations which accelerate achievement of the mission.	Staying in touch with advancements in technology and experimenting makes the organization a trendsetter for other nonprofits.	

COMPONENT 6: GROWTH AND SUSTAINABILITY

To what extent is the organization positioned for growth and sustainability?

Capacity Element	Not Active	Phase One	Phase Two	Phase Three	Phase Four	Capacity Rating
Growth		Effective activities and good relationships attract new involvement each year.	More and more people are attracted to participate in the organization's activities. Those participating in the organization experience transformation.	Plans for growth each year. Mobilizing and developing new leaders to oversee work. Vibrancy of the organization contagious.	Reproducible models lead to sustained growth. Comprehensive and integrated systems for leader development.	
Entrepreneurialism and Innovation		Activities mostly the same as other organizations with similar missions.	Evaluate effectiveness of activities and strategize to improve each year. Attract entrepreneurs.	Experiment with new approaches to activities and new programs. Evaluate to find and implement effective activities.	Culture of entrepreneurialism leads to new, effective innovations for activities and programs. Entrepreneurs regularly strategize to address opportunities and challenges.	
Funding		Ministry activities primarily resourced through relationships of the leaders.	Yearly, effective fundraising plans. Media/materials developed for fundraising.	Broad-based funding (majority revenue from small donations, followed by major donations, grants, gifts-in-kind, etc.).	Long-term strategy and plan for resource development implemented, involving board, staff, volunteers and contextually appropriate other sources.	
Program Sustainability		Barely adequate resources (people and funds) with responses geared to immediate needs. Understand programs means to accomplish the vision.	Sufficient financial and human resources, adequate program management and measurable positive impact.	Long-term sustainability ensured through ongoing mobilization of people and other resources.	Programs reproducible in many contexts. Substantial impact achieved, which increases mobilization. Resource plan to meet present and future program requirements.	
Relationships with Community		Limited visibility and credibility.	Increased visibility and credibility through engagement with the community.	Increased public awareness achieved through widespread engagement with key constituencies and strategic alliances.	Organization provides leadership in educating the public, resulting in the shaping of attitudes, policies and actions.	

NOTES

CHAPTER 1: A VISION TO FLOURISH

[1] When I use the word "organization," I have in mind entities such as churches, mission agencies, NGOs, nonprofits, commercial enterprises and businesses. These may be used interchangeably with "organizations."

[2] Barbara L. Fredrickson and Marcial F. Losada, "Positive Affect and the Complex Dynamics of Human Flourishing," *American Psychologist* 60, no.7 (October 2005): 678.

[3] Corey L.M. Keyes, "The Mental Health Continuum: From Languishing to Flourishing in Life," *Journal of Health and Social Behavior* 43, no.2 (June 2002): 209, 211.

[4] Andy Crouch, in *Playing God: Redeeming the Gift of Power*, defines the image of God as "the unique role that human beings play in representing the cosmos's Creator in the midst of creation" ([Downers Grove, IL: InterVarsity Press, 2013], 12).

[5] Patrick Lencioni's definition of organizational health adds specific contours

to flourishing organizations. An organization is healthy if there are "minimal politics and confusion, high degrees of morale and productivity, and very low turnover among good employees." Patrick Lencioni, *The Advantage: Why Organizational Health Trumps Everything Else in Business* (San Francisco: Jossey-Bass, 2012), 5.

[6] Ronald A. Heifitz and Marty Linsky, *Leadership on the Line: Staying Alive through the Dangers of Leading* (Boston: Harvard Business School Press, 2002), 13.

[7] James Collins, *Good to Great: Why Some Companies Make the Leap ... and Others Don't* (New York: HarperBusiness, 2001), 14.

[8] Ronald Heifetz, Alexander Grashow and Marty Linsky, *The Practice of Adaptive Leadership: Tools and Tactics for Changing Your Organization and the World* (Boston: Harvard Business School Press, 2009), 14.

CHAPTER 2: LANGUISHING OR FLOURISHING?

[1] Steve Stuckey, "The Official Campus by the Sea Problem Solver's Guide," www.campusbythesea.org/stories/official-campus-s

ea-problem-solver's-guide. This rendition and summary of the story is from Andy Le Peau, "Stuckey's Axiom," in his blog *Andy Unedited,* November 13, 2009, http://andyunedited.ivpress.com/2009/11/stuckeys_axiom.php, and is used by permission.

[2] See seminal work from Peter Senge, *The Fifth Discipline: The Art and Practice of the Learning Organization,* revised and updated ed. (New York: Doubleday, 2006).

[3] Ronald Heifetz, Alexander Grashow and Marty Linsky, *The Practice of Adaptive Leadership: Tools and Tactics for Changing Your Organization and the World* (Boston: Harvard Business School Press, 2009), 32.

[4] J. Robert Clinton, *The Making of a Leader: Recognizing the Lessons and Stages of Leadership Development,* 2nd ed. (Colorado Springs: NavPress, 2012), 10.

CHAPTER 3: THE ECO MODEL AT WORK

[1] Ronald A. Heifetz and Marty Linsky, *Leadership on the Line: Staying Alive through the Dangers of Leading* (Boston: Harvard Business School Press, 2002), 13.

[2] Acme is not based on any particular organization but is a fictionalized composite.

CHAPTER 4: FLOURISHING PEOPLE

[1] Africa Future is a fictional organization.
[2] I created this vignette from a story Max De Pree told me while interviewing him for a research project in 1999. Max De Pree is the former CEO and chairman of Herman Miller, Inc., a state-of-the-art office furniture company in Zeeland, Michigan.
[3] Andy Crouch, *Playing God: Redeeming the Gift of Power* (Downers Grove, IL: InterVaristy Press, 2013), 12.
[4] Chris Wienand, former pastor of Southlands Church, Brea, CA, http://southlands.net.
[5] Stephen Seamands, *Ministry in the Image of God: The Trinitarian Shape of Christian Service* (Downers Grove, IL: InterVarsity Press, 2005), 33.
[6] Colin Gunton, quoted in Seamands, *Ministry in the Image of God*, 35.
[7] Many of these ideas were first developed for "A Theology for Transcending Culture

in Leadership: The Mission of God in Conversation with the Cultural Dimension of Power Distance," *Journal of Religious Leadership* 12, no.1 (Spring 2013).

[8] Augustine, *On the Trinity*, 8.10.14, trans. Arthur West Haddon, vol.3, first series of *The Nicene and Post-Nicene Fathers*, reprinted ed. (Grand Rapids: Eerdmans, 1980), 124, quoted in Stanley J. Grenz, *Rediscovering the Triune God: The Trinity in Contemporary Theology* (Minneapolis: Fortress Press, 2004), 9.

[9] Alister E. McGrath, *Christian Theology: An Introduction*, 3rd ed. (Oxford: Blackwell Publishing, 2001), 272.

[10] Catherine LaCugna, "The Relational God: Aquinas and Beyond," *Theological Studies* 46 (1985): 650, 654.

[11] Quoted in Grenz, *Recovering the Triune God*, 81.

[12] Leonardo Boff, quoted in ibid., 121.

[13] Warren S. Brown and Brad D. Strawn, *The Physical Nature of the Christian Life: Neuroscience, Psychology, and the Church* (Cambridge: Cambridge University Press, 2012), kindle location 1618.

[14] Daniel Goleman, Richard Boyatzis and Annie McKee, *Primal Leadership: Realizing the Power of Emotional Intelligence* (Boston:

Harvard Business School Press, 2002), 6.
[15] Ibid., 7.
[16] Daniel Goleman and Richard Boyatzis, "Social Intelligence and the Biology of Leadership," *Harvard Business Review*, September 2008, 76.
[17] Goleman, Boyatzis and McKee, *Primal Leadership*, 6.
[18] See Goleman, *Emotional Intelligence: Why It Can Matter More than IQ* (New York: Bantam Books, 2005); *Primal Leadership*; and "Social Intelligence."
[19] Goleman, Boyatzis and McKee, *Primal Leadership*, 5.
[20] Ibid.
[21] Barbara L. Fredrickson and Marcial F. Losada, "Positive Affect and the Complex Dynamics of Human Flourishing," *American Psychologist* 60, no.7 (October 2005): 678.
[22] Goleman, Boyatzis and McKee, *Primal Leadership*, 14.
[23] "Organizational cultures are created by leaders, and one of the most decisive functions of leadership may well be the creation, the management, and—if and when that may become necessary—the destruction of culture." Edgar H. Schein,

Organizational Culture and Leadership (San Francisco: Jossey-Bass, 1985), 2.

[24] Goleman, Boyatzis and McKee, *Primal Leadership*, 36.
[25] Ibid., 47.
[26] See Goleman, *Emotional Intelligence*.
[27] Grenz, *Recovering the Triune God*, 79.
[28] Veli-Matti Kärkkäinen, *The Trinity: Global Perspectives* (Louisville: Westminster John Knox Press, 2007), 108.
[29] Grenz, *Recovering the Triune God*, 80.
[30] Quoted in Seamands, *Ministry in the Image of God*, 34.
[31] Mirsolav Volf, *After Our Likeness: The Church as the Image of the Trinity* (Grand Rapids: Eerdmans, 1998), 232.
[32] Robert Banks and Bernice Ledbetter, *Reviewing Leadership: A Christian Evaluation of Current Approaches* (Grand Rapids: Baker Academic, 2004), 86.

CHAPTER 5: DNA: THE LIFE FORCE OF FLOURISHING ORGANIZATIONS

[1] Patrick Lencioni encourages leadership teams and all people in the organization to have clarity regarding these questions:

"1) Why do we exist? 2) How do we behave? 3) What do we do? 4) How will we succeed? 5) What is most important right now? 6) Who must do what?" Patrick Lencioni, *The Advantage: Why Organizational Health Trumps Everything Else in Business* (San Francisco: Jossey-Bass, 2012), 77.

[2] Ronald Heifetz, Alexander Grashow and Marty Linsky, *The Practice of Adaptive Leadership: Tools and Tactics for Changing Your Organization and the World* (Boston: Harvard Business School Press, 2009), 14.

[3] For this chapter, keep in mind that values is in a constant feedback loop with faith assumptions—theological beliefs either espoused or not.

[4] Collins and Porras use the phrase "core ideology" similarly where core ideology is a combination of "core values, ... the organization's essential and enduring tenets—a small set of general guiding principles; not to be confused with specific cultural or operating practices; not to be compromised for financial gain or short-term expediency" and "purpose, ... the organization's fundamental reasons for existence beyond just making money—a perpetual guiding star on the horizon; not

to be confused with specific goals or business strategies." James C. Collins and Jerry I. Porras, *Built to Last: Successful Habits of Visionary Companies* (New York: Harper Business, 2002), 73.

[5] "Mission" is also often identified as an organization's purpose—the reason for which it exists. It is important to know and embrace the purpose! Make sure also to identify what the organization does.

[6] Aubrey Malphurs likens vision to a "telescope. It brings the distant horizon—the destination—into clear view." Aubrey Malphurs, *Values-Driven Leadership: Discovering and Developing Your Core Values for Ministry* (Grand Rapids: Baker Books, 1996), 32.

CHAPTER 6: PUTTING YOUR DNA TO WORK

[1] A SWOT analysis is the articulation of an organization's strengths and weaknesses and its context's opportunities and threats.

[2] James C. Collins and Jerry I. Porras, *Built to Last: Successful Habits of Visionary Companies* (New York: HarperBusiness, 2002), 24, 79.

CHAPTER 7: THE DISCIPLINE OF FLOURISHING—ORGANIZATION AND CAPACITY DEVELOPMENT

[1] Conversation with author, June 2013.
[2] Brené Brown, "The Power of Vulnerability," June 2010, www.ted.com/talks/brene_brown_on_vulnerability?language=en.

CHAPTER 8: MAKING ORGANIZATION DEVELOPMENT WORK FOR YOU

[1] Max De Pree, *Leadership Jazz: The Essential Elements of a Great Leader*, revised ed. (New York: Crown Business, 2008), 2.
[2] The International Council is a triennial gathering of all of OMF's directors. Decisions for strategic directions and overall policy are taken in this gathering.

CHAPTER 9: THE ECOSYSTEM OF FLOURISHING—CULTURE

[1] Edgar H. Schein, *Organizational Culture and Leadership* (San Francisco: Jossey-Bass, 1985), 9.
[2] Ibid., 2.
[3] Ibid., 14-15, 18.
[4] James C. Collins and Jerry I. Porras, *Built to Last: Successful Habits of Visionary Companies* (New York: HarperBusiness, 2002), 122.
[5] Schein, *Organizational Culture and Leadership*, 224-25.

CHAPTER 11: THE ECOSYSTEM OF FLOURISHING—STRUCTURE

[1] Henry Mintzberg, *Structure in Fives: Designing Effective Organizations* (Englewood Cliffs, NJ: Prentice Hall, 1983), 2.
[2] Ibid., 3.
[3] "Silo mentality: A mind-set present in some companies when certain departments or sectors do not wish to share information with others in the same company. This type of mentality will reduce the efficiency of the overall

operation, reduce morale, and may contribute to the demise of a productive company culture." BusinessDictionary.com, accessed February 1, 2013, www.businessdictionary.com/definition/silo-mentality.html.

CHAPTER 12: THE NUTS AND BOLTS OF STRUCTURE

[1] Mintzberg's theory offers five elements of structure: (1) operating core—members of the organization who do the essential work of the organization's purpose; (2) strategic apex—those who ensure the mission is accomplished and provide accountability to constituencies; (3) middle line—middle managers who connect the operating core with the strategic apex; (4) technostructure—analysts who help the organization do the work more effectively and efficiently; (5) support staff—members who enable the work through processes such as accounting, human resource procedures, administration, etc. Henry Mintzberg, *Structure in Fives: Designing Effective Organizations* (Englewood Cliffs, NJ: Prentice Hall, 1983), 12-16.

[2] Max De Pree shared this approach with me in 1999 while I interviewed him for a research project.

[3] Pat Lencioni's *Death by Meetings: A Leadership Fable ... About Solving the Most Painful Problem in Business* (San Francisco: Jossey-Bass, 2004) offers insight for the purpose and structure of meetings.

CHAPTER 13: THE FUTURE OF FLOURISHING—INNOVATION AND ENTREPRENEURS

[1] Paul Pierson, *The Dynamics of Christian Mission: History Through a Missiological Perspective* (Pasadena: William Carey International University Press, 2009).

[2] Ichak Adizes, *Managing Corporate Lifecycles* (Santa Barbara: Adizes Institute Publications, 2004), 112, 117.

[3] James C. Collins and Jerry I. Porras, *Built to Last: Successful Habits of Visionary Companies* (New York: HarperBusiness, 2002), 82.

[4] "D" stands for Dominance, meaning an "emphasis on shaping the environment by overcoming opposition to accomplish results." "I" stands for Influence, meaning

an "emphasis on shaping the environment by influencing or persuading others." "S" stands for Steadiness, meaning an "emphasis on cooperating with others within existing circumstances to carry out the task." "C" stands for Conscientiousness, meaning an "emphasis on working conscientiously within existing circumstances to ensure quality and accuracy." Both D and C are more task focused personalities, and I and S more relational. "DiSC Overview," accessed July 6, 2012, www.discprofile.com/whatisdisc.htm.

[5] Pat Lencioni, *The Five Dysfunctions of a Team: A Leadership Fable* (San Francisco: Jossey-Bass, 2002). Lencioni characterizes the five dysfunctions as (1) absence of trust, which leads to (2) fear of conflict, which leads to (3) lack of commitment, which leads to (4) avoidance of accountability, which leads to (5) inattention to results.

[6] I first learned this approach in Bill Thrall, Bruce McNicol and Ken McElrath, *The Ascent of a Leader: How Ordinary Relationships Develop Extraordinary Character and Influence* (San Francisco: Jossey-Bass, 1999).

[7] Etienne C. Wenger and William M. Snyder, "Communities of Practice: The Organizational Frontier," *Harvard Business Review*, January 2000, 139.

[8] International Foundation for Action Learning, "How Action Learning Works," accessed August 16, 2014, http://ifal.org.uk/action-learning/how-action-learning-works/.

CHAPTER 14: FLOURISHING: A DAILY REALITY

[1] James Collins, *Good to Great: Why Some Companies Make the Leap ... and Others Don't* (San Francisco: HarperBusiness, 2001), 95-96.

[2] Collins normally uses the phrase "economic engine" for this question; however, for the social sector he offers "resource engine," knowing that in the noncommercial context, effective means do not just relate to finances but to people, volunteers, partners, as well as money. "Good to Great and the Social Sectors," accessed August 15, 2013, www.jimcollins.com/books/g2g-ss.html.

CHAPTER 15: ONE ORGANIZATION'S STORY

[1] Mission of Prison Fellowship International: *Engaging the Christian community to pursue justice and healing in response to crime to the end that offenders are transformed, relationships are reconciled, and communities are restored.* Vision of Prison Fellowship International: *A reconciling community of restoration for all involved in or affected by crime, thereby proclaiming and demonstrating the redemptive love and transforming power of Jesus Christ for all people.* "Who We Are," accessed September 18, 2014, https://pfi.org/who-we-are/.

[2] Bruce Wydick, "Want to Change the World? Sponsor a Child," *Christianity Today*, June 14, 2013, www.christianitytoday.com/ct/2013/june/want-to-change-world-sponsor-child.html?paging=off.

[3] "Christianity Explored is an independent UK Charity which originated at All Souls Church, Langham Place, London.... We produce courses and other materials to help people understand from the Bible who Jesus is, why he came, and what it means to follow him." "About Us,"

accessed September 27, 2014, www.chris tianityexplored.org/about-us.

CHAPTER 16: FLOURISHING ORGANIZATIONS

[1] Figure 16.1 was created by Alison Clarkson Webb.

[2] Note: if they are positional leaders, they are more likely to have the characteristics of what Collins labels "Level 5" leadership—a blend of humility and tenacious will. Level 5 leaders place the good of the organization and people over and above their egos. They have a developmental, flourishing mindset directed toward individuals and the organization as a whole. Interestingly, they are not charismatic, public figures, and actually if there is "the presence of a gargantuan personal ego" it contributes "to the demise or continued mediocrity of the company." James Collins, *Good to Great: Why Some Companies Make the Leap ... and Others Don't* (New York: HarperBusiness, 2001), 22, 29.

[3] Note: because procedures and operations are so individual to the needs and contexts of different organizations, I will

not address them beyond the description in this chapter.

APPENDIX I: TECHNICAL ASPECTS OF FLOURISHING

[1] Corey L.M. Keyes, "Promoting and Protecting Mental Health as Flourishing: A Complementary Strategy for Improving National Mental Health," *American Psychologist* 62, no.2 (Feb./Mar. 2007): 95.

[2] Ibid.

[3] Barbara L. Fredrickson and Marcial F. Losada, "Positive Affect and the Complex Dynamics of Human Flourishing," *American Psychologist* 60, no.7 (Oct. 2005): 678.

[4] Corey L.M. Keyes, "The Mental Health Continuum: From Languishing to Flourishing in Life," *Journal of Health and Social Behavior* 43, no.2 (June 2002): 209.

[5] Ibid., 211.

[6] Barbara L. Fredrickson, "What Good Are Positive Emotions?" *Review of General Psychology* 2, no.3 (1998): 304.

[7] Andy Crouch defines the image of God as "the unique role that human beings play in representing the cosmos's Creator in the midst of creation" in *Playing God:*

Redeeming the Gift of Power (Downers Grove, IL: InterVarsity Press, 2013), 12.

[8] Note: when I use the word "organization," I have in mind entities such as churches, mission agencies, NGOs, nonprofits, commercial enterprises and businesses. These may be used interchangeably with "organizations."

[9] Patrick Lencioni's definition of organizational health adds specific contours to flourishing organizations. An organization is healthy if there are "minimal politics and confusion, high degrees of morale and productivity, and very low turnover among good employees." Patrick Lencioni, *The Advantage: Why Organizational Health Trumps Everything Else in Business* (San Francisco: Jossey-Bass, 2012), 5.

Index

A
action learning, *126, 205, 206, 208*
action plans, *92, 93, 107, 248*
adaptive leadership, *9, 15*
asset (mapping), *222, 245, 246*

B
budget, budgeting, *1, 19, 64, 79, 92, 95, 102, 107, 109, 111, 122, 165, 173, 201*

C
Campus by the Sea, *11, 13*
change (dynamics), *2, 7, 9, 11, 13, 14, 15, 21, 22, 28, 30, 31, 33, 34, 79, 106, 107, 122, 156, 160, 163, 172, 176, 189, 190, 206, 208, 239*
China Inland Mission, *77, 111*
communities of practice, *203, 205*

E
ECO model, *15, 17, 22, 24, 25, 27, 30, 31, 34*
emotional intelligence, *48, 50, 211*
Enterprise Rental Cars, *111*
evaluation, *19, 92, 93, 95, 104, 106, 107, 122, 124, 131, 168, 170, 181, 187, 190, 203, 208, 239, 245, 248*

F
Fuller Theological Seminary, *109, 165*
   School of Psychology, *165*
   School of Theology, *109, 165*
   School of World Mission (School of Intercultural Studies), *109, 165, 192*

G
goals, *34, 76, 92, 93, 95, 107, 109, 131, 178, 190, 210, 211, 215, 225, 227, 229, 230, 246, 248*

H
Habitat for Humanity, *71*
Herman Miller, Inc., *39, 53*
Hewlett-Packard, *87*

J
Junction, The (Mercy Town), *84*

K
Kiva, *71*

M
Max De Pree, *39, 53, 122, 186*
mission drift, *97, 99*

O
OMF International, *77, 85, 111, 119, 124, 128*
outcomes, *2, 15, 69, 70, 109, 128, 129, 170, 172, 176, 208, 216, 218, 227, 230, 232, 237, 246, 248, 249*
outputs, *225, 227*

P
planning, *19, 92, 95, 109, 111, 122, 131, 153, 165, 173, 187, 227, 229, 230, 246*
    action plans, *92, 93, 107*
Prison Fellowship International (PFI), *197, 231, 232, 234*

S
Saddleback Church, *114*
strategy, strategies, *7, 30, 58, 73, 76, 77, 90, 93, 101, 111, 114, 119, 122, 126, 158, 164, 175, 186, 189, 197, 205, 206, 221, 224, 225, 229, 236, 246, 248*
    development, *206, 215, 218, 222*
SWOT analysis, *85, 221, 222*
systems, *46, 69, 106, 123, 126, 131, 163, 181, 187, 194, 197, 198, 206, 210*
    thinking, *13, 58*

T
Trinitarian theology, *51*
Trinity, *39, 44, 45, 51, 53, 54, 56, 59*

V
vision drift, *64, 80*

W
World Vision, *71*

www.ingramcontent.com/pod-product-compliance
Lightning Source LLC
Chambersburg PA
CBHW011719220426
43663CB00018B/2921